A WALK IN MY SHOES

A WALK IN MY SHOES

Questions I'm Often Asked
as a Gay Latter-day Saint

BEN SCHILATY

DESERET
BOOK

Dedicated to Mitch and Craig—
the first people I invited to walk in my shoes,
and two of the finest men I've ever known.

Library of Congress Cataloging-in-Publication Data

CIP on file

ISBN 978-1-62972-853-7

Printed in the United States of America
LSC Communications, Crawfordsville, IN

10 9 8 7 6 5 4 3 2 1

TABLE OF CONTENTS

TABLE OF CONTENTS

PROLOGUE

Coming to Hearken

Rhoda was a young woman in the Church of Jesus Christ in the meridian of time who likely would have been lost to history had she not answered a knock at the door. Peter, the President of the Church, had just been miraculously freed from prison by an angel. Only Peter, the guards, and the heavens knew Peter was free. He arrived at a house where many of the disciples were worshipping and knocked on the door of the gate. Rhoda heard the knock, and she "came to hearken. . . . And when she knew Peter's voice, she opened not the gate for gladness, but ran in, and told how Peter stood before the gate" (Acts 12:13–14). But no one believed her. How could she be right? Peter was in prison, and they all knew that. Obviously Rhoda, this young Christian woman, had to be mistaken.

First they told her, "Thou art mad. But she constantly affirmed that it was even so" (Acts 12:15). When she persisted, the people dismissed what she was saying. They tried to fit her experience into their paradigm of what they knew to be true—that it couldn't be the real Peter. "Then said they, It is his angel" (v. 15). They shifted from disbelieving her account to rationalizing away what she knew she had heard.

While this dismissing and rationalizing was happening inside,

Peter was still standing at the door knocking. Finally someone realized that whoever was outside was still knocking "and when they had opened the door, and saw him, they were astonished" (v. 16). When they saw with their own eyes what Rhoda had been telling them all along, they believed. Her words didn't convince them, but their personal experience did.

I don't blame the people for not believing Rhoda. She was saying something that was contrary to what they knew. How could she possibly be right? But she was right. What she had said was the truth.

The whole story might have been different if all of them "came to hearken," as Rhoda did, the first time Peter knocked on the door. But she had been the only one who went out to listen and attend to the person knocking at the door. And because of that, Peter was left outside knocking while they argued inside about whether or not he was really there.

I have experienced something similar as I have told people that I'm gay. Someone who doesn't believe me will say, "You're not gay. A loving God wouldn't do that to anyone." My orientation doesn't fit into their paradigm and therefore cannot be real. When this happens, I am put in the uncomfortable position of having to "constantly affirm" that what I'm saying is real. Fortunately, these reactions have been few. Most people believe me when I tell them what I have experienced, but it has also been very common for people to dismiss the implications of my reality.

My parents, who are true heroes in my life, initially responded in a less than ideal way when I came out to them at the age of twenty-three. I didn't consider myself gay back then. I was "more attracted to men than women." My parents responded immediately with love and concern, making sure that I knew they loved me. My mom asked if it was a phase, and I said, "I hope so." She then told me that once I had a girlfriend, the feelings would go way. She saw my same-sex attraction as the result of inexperience—that more experience with the opposite sex would right the thing in me that was wrong.

One of the first things my dad said was, "Well, you're probably better off being single, because being married is hard." "Things could be worse, so be grateful for what you've got" was frequent advice from him. I count it as one of the great blessings of my life that my mom and my dad didn't stick with their initial assessment of the situation. They continued to listen, and as their understanding increased, their perspectives shifted. When they saw what I saw, they no longer tried to explain away what I felt.

I have seen this happen again and again. When people begin to recognize what their LGBTQ loved ones are feeling and experiencing, their hearts begin to expand. I saw this happen when I gave a stake fireside on how to minister to LGBTQ Latter-day Saints. During the Q&A, an older woman grabbed the microphone. With a shaky voice, she said, "I don't have a question, but I want you to know that I came here tonight believing that being gay is a choice and now I know that it's not. Thank you for teaching me that." And she then passed the mic to someone else.

Much like Rhoda, I know what it's like to not be believed and to have my experiences explained away. I am not asking you to simply believe my words. And I don't blame you if you have trouble accepting what I have to say. But I am inviting you to see what I have seen and experience what I have experienced. I'm inviting you to put on my shoes and walk around in them. I wear size 13, so they may feel a little uncomfortable at first and likely won't fit right. And you may stumble in them a bit. That's okay, I've stumbled in my shoes, too. I invite you to come and hearken. Come to the door and see who is knocking.

INTRODUCTION

Expanding the Borders of Zion

Dear brothers and sisters, we belong to each other.
We can be "knit together in unity and in love"
(Mosiah 18:21) in all things and in all places.

–GERRIT W. GONG, "Christ the Lord Is Risen Today," *Ensign*, May 2018

Being a gay Latter-day Saint is a peculiar space to be in. I grew up in a time and place where it wasn't okay to be gay or a Latter-day Saint. Yet I ended up being both. I loved my religious convictions with a fervor that surely annoyed my friends and non-Latter-day-Saint relatives who patiently listened when I preached at them. My teachers were kind enough to allow me to do class presentations on the Nauvoo Temple and feign interest in my book reports on The Work and the Glory series. All of my friends would have said I was super Mormon (a word that was okay to use back in the '90s). But I was also attracted to other boys. And I was taught that was not okay. I embraced the spiritual part of myself as much as I could while simultaneously hiding my orientation. The latter half of that changed in January 2015, when I came out on my blog. Then that November I spoke publicly for the first time about my faith and my sexuality. Exposing some of the deepest parts of myself to a chapel full of people was a terrifying thing to do.

Brother Bauer, the director of the Tucson Institute of Religion, had asked me to speak on my experiences as a gay member of the Church, which was a pretty gutsy thing for him to do. I didn't prepare any written remarks but arrived at the institute two hours before Friday devotional was to begin. I spent those two hours reading, praying, and listening to music to put myself in a place where the Spirit could speak through me. As I stood at the podium, I began my talk in a way that was completely unplanned. After telling a joke I had just thought of, I said, "Even though Brother Bauer said I'm here to talk about my experiences as a gay member of the Church, I'm really here to talk about the Atonement of Jesus Christ."

I then spoke of friends who had borne my burdens with me, times when I had wanted to give up, women I had dated, losing hope and finding it again. I shared the story of my dad giving me a blessing telling me that I would be saved in the highest degree of the celestial kingdom. My reaction to that pronouncement had been, "Oh, shoot!" because that meant that I'd be married to a woman for all eternity, and that did not sound like heaven to me.

Brother Bauer had asked to take the last few minutes of the meeting—I assume to put out any fires that I may have started by speaking so candidly about my faith and my orientation. As I sat down and he stood up, he said that he had planned on reading some quotes, but that didn't feel important anymore. Then he got emotional and said, "I want everyone to know how much I love and admire Ben. It takes a lot of faith to hope and trust in promises that you don't even want."

I am in such a peculiar space. I believe in modern prophets and the Book of Mormon and the Atonement of Jesus Christ and eternal families and everything that comes in the package of the Restoration. And yet, what I know of exaltation—including being sealed to a woman for eternity—doesn't sound that great to me. But I'm still working towards being exalted in the eyes of God. I'm walking a covenant path that has as its destination a form of eternity that I'm not sure I even want. But I'm walking it because I feel called to do so.

I am sharing these stories in an attempt to follow President M. Russell Ballard's counsel. He said, "We need to listen to and understand what our LGBT brothers and sisters are feeling and experiencing. Certainly we must do better than we have done in the past so that all members feel they have a spiritual home where their brothers and sisters love them and where they have a place to worship and serve the Lord."[1] I love this apostolic invitation to listen and understand along with the acknowledgment that we must do better than we have been doing.

The Lord defines Zion in part as a people "of one heart and one mind" (Moses 7:18). I don't think this means that we must all think and feel the same things, but that we strive to understand what is in one another's hearts and minds. In order to do this we have to be vulnerable with each other. Openness builds trust, trust builds unity, and unity builds Zion. I believe that as we open up to one another, we can expand the borders of Zion and grow into the people that God would have us be. I hope that we will build Zion together as I invite you into my heart in the pages that follow.

If you read these stories and feel hopeful and optimistic about me and my life—thank you. I'm hopeful and optimistic about my life, too. My life is good and full and wonderful and I love the way that I'm living it. However, my life is my own, and my experiences shouldn't be generalized to anyone else. My biggest fear in sharing my life is that someone will say to a gay loved one, "Hey, I just read this awesome book by Ben Schilaty, and you can do what he does and be just like him!" I would hate it if that happened. I don't want anyone to try to be like me. I don't want to be anyone's poster boy. I live in unique, peculiar circumstances, and I don't expect anyone to make the choices I make. Telling someone to do what I do is like taking my glasses off of my face, handing them to someone else, and saying, "Here, these should help." All that would do for your loved ones is give them blurry vision and a headache. That said, I do hope to share some important principles that have guided me on my gay Latter-day Saint journey. If you feel the need to point your gay loved one to an exemplar, point them to Jesus Christ and His attributes.

I'd like to start this book the same way I started my talk at the Tucson Institute. As I spoke that day, I felt inspired to say something that I had never articulated before: "I used to think that the Atonement of Jesus Christ would make me straight, but instead it healed my broken heart." We all have broken parts in us. We all have pain and disappointment. We all experience sorrow and grief. So as you walk this peculiar road with me, my hope is that you will walk away with a greater understanding of the Atonement of Jesus Christ.

HE HAS SENT ME HERE

Were you born gay?

If you will always keep in mind that you are actually the children of your Heavenly Father, that there is something of Him in you, and that you may aspire to become something like that from which you came and cooperate with Him in the unfinished work of creation, you will remember that His plan for the salvation of His children had purpose behind it—a design to be carried out. If you keep these great truths in mind, you will be fortified and sustained, whatever life may hold for you.

—HUGH B. BROWN, "God Is the Gardener" (Brigham Young University devotional, May 31, 1968)

My parents are super rad. I think that's how Nephi would have started the Book of Mormon had he been born in Everett, Washington, in 1984. If you were to spend time with them, you'd come away saying that Ginny Schilaty is an angel (because she is) and that Buzz Schilaty is delightfully charming (because he is). My parents are also pioneers. In a series of events worthy of an *Ensign* article, my parents joined the Church a year after they got married. They were the first members in both of their families. It was a bold and courageous thing for them to do.

When they first got married, my parents were both teachers,

and since they had to deal with children all day at work they didn't want to deal with them at home, too. So they decided not to have kids. But joining the Church and understanding the plan of salvation changed their minds, and they had three children: Jessen, Jay, and Lindsay. Three was a good number, and they decided to stop there—and then I came along. I'm what you might call an "accident" or an "oops baby" or (if you're a little more polite) an "unplanned pregnancy."

Challenges began right away. My parents weren't doing well financially, and this was not a convenient time to have another baby. Then in the fifth month of my mom's pregnancy, they learned that something was terribly wrong. The doctor told them that there was a very small chance that I would survive to full term, and that if I did survive, I would be mentally and physically disabled for my entire life. He also told them that continuing the pregnancy put my mom's life in danger and that she likely wouldn't survive. As a medical professional, he recommended that my parents abort the pregnancy.

My parents understood that according to Church teachings, terminating such a pregnancy was a matter of personal revelation. There may even be people reading this story who have wrestled with this very choice. I have the utmost respect for parents who have had to make difficult decisions regarding their families, and I'm not saying what anyone should or shouldn't do. Each circumstance is unique, and this is my parents' story.

My mom was understandably distraught. She didn't feel right terminating the pregnancy, but she didn't want to die. She and my dad visited additional doctors, talked the decision over with their parents, and counseled with a Church leader. The consensus was to abort the pregnancy. Rather than face the reality of this heart-wrenching decision, my mom just pretended that I didn't exist. Denial is a powerful coping mechanism, and it allowed her to postpone the decision until guidance came from heaven. Driving alone in the car one day she received an undeniable witness from the Spirit. She heard a voice speak to her so clearly that she thought it had come through the radio: "Benjamin Schilaty. His name will be Benjamin Schilaty." This experience gave her the courage she needed to move forward. She told my dad what had happened, and they agreed to continue with the pregnancy.

My parents had some tough conversations as they decided what to do. My mom told my dad that she was willing to give her life so that I could have a chance of being born. My dad promised my mom that if she died and I lived, he would willingly push me around in a wheelchair for the rest of his life. This is the heritage of love that I come from—two parents willing to literally give up their lives for their child. My parents exemplify this teaching of the Savior: "Greater love hath no man than this, that a man lay down his life for his friends" (John 15:13).

When my mom tells this story, she focuses on all the Relief Society sisters who ministered to my family during the forty-five days she was on bed rest in a Seattle hospital. A woman from the ward drove an hour round-trip to visit my mom every day. Relief Society sisters in the ward rotated bringing the family food. These same women would come over to clean the house—my dad would say that he could handle things on his own only to have them politely push by him and clean anyway. Two sisters regularly drove my three siblings all the way to Seattle so they could visit my mom and my dad could get some sleep.

I was born more than a month early, and on the day of the delivery there was a team of doctors in the room expecting the very worst. Contrary to the dire predictions, there were no complications. No physical disability, no mental deficits, no deaths.

My dad says that when I was born healthy and whole, the doctor held me up by my legs and said, "And to think they wanted to abort this beautiful baby."

I tell this story because I often get asked, "Were you born gay?" I don't think that's the right question. The better question is: "Did I come to earth the way my Heavenly Parents intended me to be?" To that question I can answer with a firm yes! In many of the father's blessings I've received throughout the years, my dad has said that I'm "a child of promise." Medical professionals thought I would come one way or not at all, but I came to earth exactly the way God intended me to be.

What I also know is that I did not choose to be gay. In fact, I have actively tried throughout my life not to be gay. I have prayed thousands of times to have my attractions change. And while God typically answers my prayers pretty well, He hasn't answered this one even a little. This is a fact that I have pondered extensively. I don't know all the answers, but what I do know is that God loves me. And He sent me to a home where I would be loved by parents who were willing to sacrifice their lives for me when all they knew was that I was a child of God who needed a chance to live.

QUIET IN MY CLOSET

When did you know you were gay?

*When we give our heart to the Father and the Son, we
change our world—even if circumstances around us do
not change. We draw closer to Heavenly Father and feel
His tender acceptance of our efforts to be true disciples of
Christ. Our discernment, confidence, and faith increase.*

–NEILL F. MARRIOTT, "Abiding in God and
Repairing the Breach," *Ensign*, Nov. 2017

"Are you gay, Ben?"

I experienced the question as a slap to the face. It both stung
and left me feeling exposed. To add to my distress, the question
had come at a Church activity and from a young woman I didn't
know well. I adamantly told her that I wasn't gay, wanting myself
to believe it as much as I wanted her to believe it. She continued
to press while also making a case for why she thought I was gay:
my love of musicals, my poor performance in sports, and my lack
of interest in girls (except for the Golden Girls). I denied her ac-
cusations quite forcefully, worrying that others might overhear
this conversation. Then she played a card no one had played before. "Okay, you're not gay now, but you will be in the future."

"No I won't!"

"Of course you'd say that now, because you don't think you're gay. But you will be." She smirked, knowing she had won. This exchanged haunted me. I so desperately didn't want to be gay, and I was panicked that she might be right.

I definitely did not see myself as gay as an adolescent. Not even a little bit. If you asked me if I was gay (and people did) and I said no (which I did), I wouldn't be lying. My sexual orientation was not part of my identity, and I believed that the feelings I had were just a phase that would soon be over. I completely ignored my attractions and the realities of my life until I couldn't anymore.

My childhood years were comfy and simple. My oldest brother was born when my parents had been married for five years, so they'd had a lot of time just to themselves before we took over their lives. My dad jokes that since he and my mom were teachers, they made all their parenting mistakes on other people's kids. My parents are not perfect, but they parented pretty perfectly. Out of all the good parenting they did, the most re-markable is this: in my growing-up years my parents never said one rude thing to me, not even in jest. They never made fun of me or called me dumb or anything like that. I was teased plenty, but I was never demeaned. And so I grew up thinking that I was awesome and amazing, because that's what I was always told at home. And who was I to disbelieve all the affirmations they gave me? Being reared (if I wrote *raised*, my dad would say, "You *raise* goats, you *rear* children") by Buzz and Ginny Schilaty was a very special blessing.

I spent a lot of time with my dad growing up. He would take me hiking or to the beach near our house all the time. When I was little, whenever it was just the two of us in the car, my dad would share his testimony of the Book of Mormon with me as we drove through a large forested park near our house. That book had changed his life when he first read it while investigating the Church, and he wanted me to know what he knew.

I loved animals as a kid, so my dad took me to the zoo every month. He would make peanut butter and jelly sandwiches for lunch, and as we got near the zoo food court, he'd say, "Would you like a Cinnabon?" To this day, Cinnabons are my favorite food.

I first recall being attracted to other boys in sixth grade, right as puberty was setting in. I had absolutely no concept of why all the other boys at school went on and on about female celebrities and how attractive they were. It made absolutely no sense to me. The attractive male celebrities, on the other hand—I could see why someone would be drawn to look at them. But there was no way I could say that to anyone else or even admit it to myself. Noticing how other guys talked about girls was my first hint that something was different about me. It wasn't just celebrities, though. I started to be attracted to my peers. I was not an athletic kid at all. And I most certainly couldn't have been described as "conventionally attractive." But there were boys who were athletic and conventionally attractive, and I found myself drawn to them. The lie I told myself as a teenager was, "I'm not attracted to these guys. I'm just jealous of them and wish I looked like them. It's admiration, not attraction."

In my youth, I had yet to develop the spiritual confidence to approach God with what was going on in my life. It hadn't sunk in that I had no reason to be embarrassed about what I was feeling because Christ already knew exactly how I felt. Paul taught, "For we have not an high priest which cannot be touched with the feeling of our infirmities; but was in all points tempted like as we are, yet without sin. Let us therefore come boldly unto the throne of grace, that we may obtain mercy, and find grace to help in time of need" (Hebrews 4:15–16). The Savior knew exactly what I was experiencing, and He wanted me to approach His throne so that I could have grace in my time of need. But I didn't have the courage to do that. I couldn't approach His throne insecurely, much less boldly. So I just pushed my feelings aside, pretended they didn't exist, and lived without the grace and strength that He would have freely offered me in my time of need.

Kids don't have to be super clever to tease you in a way that cuts deep. Since my name is Ben and there's a foot ointment called Bengay, it didn't take too long for some people to come up with a nickname for me. I definitely didn't want to be gay, but even more than that, I didn't want people to think I was gay. Being called Ben Gay was terrifying, and I became super defensive whenever I was called that—I was not gay and it was not okay for people to even consider that I might be. So I tried hard to alter my mannerisms so I couldn't be accused of something so awful. I stopped talking with my hands (except when I was alone, talking on the phone), and my parents and siblings helped me walk in a more masculine way. We have pictures of twelve-year-old me on vacation in Florida standing like C-3PO with my elbows slightly out looking very mechanical. I had been trying to swing my arms "naturally" and hadn't quite figured it out.

While I was ignoring my attractions to guys, not being attracted to girls was actually a benefit as a closeted Latter-day Saint teen. When my friends started getting girlfriends and making out with them, I told myself, *I'm following the prophet's counsel not to steady date before my mission. I'm being righteous.* Not only did I feel good about my obedience, I was praised by Church leaders for following the *For the Strength of Youth* guidelines. I took girls on fun dates and to school dances and we had a great time. These very wholesome dates didn't include hand-holding or doorstep scenes or anything more than a polite hug. I was able to tick off all the boxes of what a good Latter-day Saint youth should do without getting pulled into the drama of dating seriously.

I was really good at doing church stuff, too. I attended seminary, read the scriptures, went on temple trips, helped plan youth conferences, and did all the things I was supposed to do. And I prayed a lot. I prayed that my relatives and friends would join the Church, that I would get into BYU, that I would know if the Book of Mormon was true, that our country would be safe, and that President Hinckley would know how to lead the Church. I poured out my heart to God in so many ways, but I never talked to Him about my sexual orientation. It didn't even occur to me to do that.

I knew I was attracted to guys, but that didn't matter. It was just a phase, I told myself. I would go on my mission, and as a reward for my service, God would fix me. It was such a foregone conclusion in my mind that I didn't even think to pray about it. That was just how things worked. I have heard a lot of other gay Latter-day Saints say that they made a deal with God that if they served a mission, He would fix them. I didn't think to make that bargain because I was sure that a natural outcome of righteous service would be an end to my unwanted attractions. I knew that I would change. When I was interviewed by my stake president for my mission, he asked me if I had lived the law of chastity. When I said I had, he congratulated me for being so faithful because so many do break the law of chastity. I was so proud of myself for staying pure.

In the MTC I poured out my heart to God. I prayed every day to have the gift of tongues because Spanish was so hard and I was terrified of going to Mexico. I believed this blessing would be granted as long as I was obedient. Back then, all missionaries were supposed to part their hair. My hair was not parted my first day in the MTC. In my first interview with my MTC branch president, he pointed this out to me. He invited, "Elder Schilaty, will you part your hair every day of your mission for the Lord?"

"Yes, President, I will."

Partway through my mission this rule changed, and we no longer had to part our hair, but I did it anyway because I'd made a promise that I would part my hair every day of my mission. That's the kind of missionary I was: the most obedient I could be.

While I was a missionary, my orientation wasn't a concern. I had two years off from thinking about dating and marriage. And I had an excuse to not talk about it. I was attracted to other missionaries now and then, but it wasn't distressing. I just used my handy rationalization and told myself that I didn't have a crush on them, I just admired them and wished I were like them. On my mission I prayed like I had never prayed before, and I saw those prayers answered swiftly and miraculously. I poured out my heart for the people I was teaching. I poured out my heart to learn to get along with difficult companions (turns out I was often the difficult one). I poured out my heart to not get sick and to speak Spanish well. I poured out my heart regularly and frequently for the people I was learning to love. When I got home from my mission, a friend from high school asked me what I'd learned in Mexico. "I learned that God hears and answers prayers," I told her. "He doesn't always answer them in the way I'd like, but He always answers them."

Looking back, it's so curious that I prayed so much about so many things, and yet I never prayed about being gay. I was ashamed of admitting this reality to God and to myself. After listing thing after thing to pray for, Amulek taught: "But this is not all; ye must pour out your souls in your closets, and your secret places, and in your wilderness" (Alma 34:26). Amulek didn't say in *the* wilderness, but in *your* wilderness. My wilderness, the place that I was too afraid to explore. The place that held my deeply guarded secret that I believed would vanish before I had to face it. The place that I really wasn't sure I could go.

And then suddenly I couldn't stay away from the wilderness anymore. I was a returned missionary, and my next duty, the next box to check off, was eternal marriage. I stood at the edge of the wilderness.

Three days after returning home from Mexico, I was watching TV by myself and some handsome, shirtless men appeared on the screen. I was intensely attracted to them, and I was disgusted with myself. And I got really scared. It hadn't worked. My mission hadn't fixed me, even though I had felt so sure it would. And so, for the first time in my life, I stepped into the wilderness. I knelt on the air mattress I was sleeping on in my parents' rec room and poured out my heart. "Heavenly Father, I think I'm gay, and I don't want to be." I shuddered a little. "Please remove these attractions I have for thy sons and replace them with attractions to thy daughters."

That young woman from my teenage years had been right. I was gay. She had seen in me something that I was unwilling to see in myself. She saw into a closet that I was unable to acknowledge existed. And now that I saw it and acknowledged it, I wanted to change it just as much as ever. In my metaphorical closet, kneeling on an air mattress, I poured out my heart to my Maker. In the secret place of my temporary bedroom, I told Him what was in my soul. For the first time in my life, I finally started talking to God about my sexual orientation. And the first thing I told Him was that I wanted to change.

CHOOSING TO BE STRAIGHT

Is being gay a choice?

Righteousness and faith certainly are instrumental in moving mountains—if moving mountains accomplishes God's purposes and is in accordance with His will. Righteousness and faith certainly are instrumental in healing the sick, deaf, and lame—if such healing accomplishes God's purposes and is in accordance with His will. Thus, even if we have strong faith, many mountains will not be moved.

–DAVID A. BEDNAR, "Accepting the Lord's
Will and Timing," *Ensign*, Aug. 2016

I was raised to be straight. My family, my culture, my religion—everything pointed me to being straight. And I wanted to be straight, too. I wanted to have a "normal" life like everyone else. I wanted to get married to a woman, have a cool family, and pass on my unique last name to the next generation. Not only did I want to be straight, but outwardly I was straight. I was making a concerted, valiant effort to like women. And aside from the cognitive dissonance going on in my head, I acted in every way like a straight man. I didn't talk about liking guys, I didn't write in my journal about it, I didn't flirt with guys, or date guys, or hold hands with them, or cuddle with them, or kiss them, or anything that a gay person might do. On the contrary, I did all that with women.

Nephi testified that if we "go and do," God will "prepare a way" for us to accomplish His commandments (1 Nephi 3:7). I felt that I was being commanded to find a wife and start my own eternal family. My mission hadn't cured me of my same-sex attraction like I thought it would, so now was the time to overcome it. I "went and did" the very best I could so that God would reward me with being attracted to a wonderful woman. I made sure that my actions were in line with my desires. It would be difficult to try harder than I did to get married. I have been on twenty-seven blind dates, and I think I've been out with more than a hundred women. The only possible life I could envision for myself was married with a family, and being gay was preventing me from keeping that commandment. There was no other way to live life than married to a woman. I was going to marry a woman. I had to. There was no other option. I thought that if I met as many women as possible, I'd be able to find the one that I was meant to be with. During one semester of college I had a goal to go out with a different woman every week. In my twenties, I spent thousands of dollars and many hundreds of hours dating women, and I was very unsuccessful. I went on so many dates, in fact, that I was regularly accused of leading girls on. Since no one knew that I was gay, it looked like I was toying with hearts.

Choosing to be straight included not just trying to get married but trying to change the core of my attractions as well. I prayed and read the scriptures every day, I wrote in my journal regularly, I attended the temple every week, I served in my calling, and I did what we used to call home teaching. I believed that if I were just righteous enough, God would fix me. Some of these practices were natural outgrowths of my faith, while some of them I did to try to earn a change in my orientation. To me, observance equaled righteousness. These practices were like deposits in a heavenly bank. Once I saved up enough righteousness, God would give me the blessing I wanted.

I found that viewing blessings transactionally left me poorer. For example, attending the temple weekly has been an important practice for me for more than a decade. Doing this has brought me countless blessings. However, I often attend the temple because I'm supposed to—to check off something on my to-do list. These are the times when I feel bored in the temple because I'm there out of obligation. Then other times I enter the temple seeking to connect with God and commune with the Divine. My temple worship isn't to show my faith; it is because of my faith. When that is my motivation, I leave feeling edified and fortified. In my experience, observing the commandments as an outcome of faith has led to much more growth than observing to receive a reward.

While there was some dissonance, discouragement, and discomfort in my early dating, it was mostly a lot of fun. Shortly after my mission I returned to BYU. So many people have found their spouses there, and I was certain I would, too. I took women hiking, we played racquetball, went stargazing, carved pumpkins and put them on our heads, and all the other normal BYU dating shenanigans. Going on dates and getting to know people was a blast, and I enjoyed it immensely. It was the trying to pair off and form a romantic relationship that took an emotional toll. I would meet and become close to these super amazing women, and then I wouldn't know what to do. I knew that as we paired off I was supposed to hold hands with them and kiss them, but that seemed so unnatural to me. The pressure I felt to be physically affectionate diminished the enjoyment of our time together. Recognizing that discomfort in myself was a reminder that I wasn't attracted to women, and that terrified me.

As part of choosing to be straight, I began to scour the BYU library for books about what causes same-sex attraction and how to correct it. There were multiple books, and I was certain I'd find an answer in them. I was terrified that if I checked out one of the books, my name would be forever linked with same-sex attraction, so I read them in the library. I'd sit in a study carrel with a few other books so if someone I knew walked by I could quickly conceal the books about homosexuality under books about Latin America. Then when I was done, I'd carefully reshelve the books and come back later. Going through these books in the quiet corners of the library became an obsession, and I neglected school assignments to find answers.

I started this study with aspirations to fix myself, because I certainly couldn't stay gay. But then I got really confused. The books discussed multiple causes of same-sex attraction: an overbearing mother and a distant father; early sexual abuse; a desire to have close relationships with men that became sexualized at puberty; a failure to connect to one's masculine side. Besides being bad at sports, none of the causes mentioned in the books described my life. However, I also read that therapy could help to correct my attractions. Maybe that would work. I made an appointment with the BYU counseling center.

I was twenty-three, and it was my first time ever in a therapist's office. I filled out what felt like stacks of papers, carefully answering each question on a questionnaire so that my therapist could help me. I wrote on one form that I wanted to become attracted to women and not men. When I walked into the therapist's office, nervous and unsure, he glanced at what I'd written on the form and said, "Well, this is easy to fix," and set the form down in a nonchalant way that felt dismissive of the gravity of the situation.

My impression of therapy from TV and movies was that I would constantly be asked, "And how does that make you feel?" That's not how this was at all. He normalized my attractions by walking me through the different parts of male and female bodies that make them attractive to people. I said very little in the session, and I felt extremely uncomfortable. He used words to describe the female anatomy that a gay and naïve Latter-day Saint like me had never heard. He also said that a lot of same-sex attraction is environmental and that it can be changed. I didn't know how to feel about that, because I couldn't think of anything that had caused this. Basically, he wasn't helpful. He went through possible causes of homosexuality, but I couldn't see how any of them applied to me.

At the end of my first session, the therapist told me that we would really get to work in the next session. So a week later I went back. He talked almost the entire session, explaining how I had developed a thought pattern of seeing an attractive man and ruminating on his attractiveness. I needed to stop doing that, he said. And instead, whenever I felt aroused, I was to think of the beautiful aspects of a woman's body. That was the answer. I just needed to train my brain to find women attractive. He gave me some homework that made me feel really uncomfortable, and I left the office and scheduled a third session because I didn't have the courage to tell him I didn't want to come back. I called the secretary later that day to cancel the appointment. I never went back. I wrote in my journal: "I felt pretty lousy afterward. I had put a lot of hope into this and it ended up being an uncomfortable waste of time."

Praying, fasting, temple attendance, dating, scripture study, therapy. I did all that I could to change. I wondered why the promise in Ether 12:27 wasn't working. The Lord told Moroni: "And if men come unto me I will show unto them their weakness. I give unto men weakness that they may be humble; and my grace is sufficient for all men that humble themselves before me; for if they humble themselves before me, and have faith in me, then will I make weak things become strong unto them." Same-sex attraction was my weakness, and I was striving to come unto Christ and be humble, so why wasn't this promise working for me? Why wasn't my weakness of being attracted to men going away?

As I studied the context of Ether 12:27 more, I began to see myself in the chapter. Moroni said, "Lord, the Gentiles will mock at these things, because of our weakness in writing" (v. 23). He continued, "I fear lest the Gentiles shall mock at our words" (v. 25). As I likened these verses to myself, I realized that I feared that my abilities weren't going to be enough. I was worried that I wouldn't be able to marry a woman. And I was worried that I would be mocked if anyone knew that I experienced same-sex attraction. After the Lord promised Moroni that He would teach the Gentiles about faith, hope, and charity, Moroni shifted from focusing on his own perceived inability to God's power to do His work: "And it came to pass that I prayed unto the Lord that he would give unto the Gentiles grace, that they might have charity" (v. 36). God took Moroni's writing and infused it with His Spirit. Moroni didn't need to be a gifted writer for God to make his writing a gift to millions of people.

Like Moroni, I initially focused on myself instead of looking outward and trusting in the Lord. How could I live with any outcome that wasn't a change in my orientation? How could God possibly use my same-sex attraction to build His kingdom? Moroni wanted people to believe his account and was concerned that his weakness would prevent that, and I wanted to become straight. My hopes had been placed on one specific outcome. The Lord told Moroni, "And because thou hast seen thy weakness thou shalt be made strong, even unto the sitting down in the place which I have prepared in the mansions of my Father" (v. 37).

Same-sex attraction wasn't my weakness. My real weakness was that I didn't trust in God's plan. God took Moroni's ability and magnified it to do His work, and Moroni developed faith, hope, and charity. Similarly, God didn't change my sexual orientation like I begged Him to. Instead, He taught me how to trust Him. As I have matured, I've seen how my sexual orientation has become the main vehicle through which I share my testimony of the Savior. My perceived weakness has become one of the ways that I work to build Zion. Just as Moroni testified in Ether, God did turn my weakness into a strength as I turned to Him.

During this time in my early twenties, becoming straight and getting married was the central focus of my life. These were not wasted years, but precious experiences that shaped me into who I am today. I wanted so much to just live a normal life with my wife and kids. I wanted to do God's will for me. Occasionally, well-meaning people will insist that being gay is a choice. The exact opposite has been true for me as I have tried as hard as I could to be straight. Choosing to be straight caused me a lot of anxiety and discomfort. I felt like I was lying to the people I was dating, and the inherent dishonesty of continually dating women I wasn't attracted to really weighed on me.

I have met many hundreds of gay Latter-day Saints, and none of them chose to be gay. In fact, most of them have similar stories to mine, in which they chose to be straight and actively tried to change their orientation for years. If people are choosing to be gay, or trying to become gay, they are in a tiny minority.

As President M. Russell Ballard taught, "The Church of Jesus Christ of Latter-day Saints believes that 'the experience of same-sex attraction is a complex reality for many people.'" He continued, "'Even though individuals do not choose to have such attractions, they do choose how to respond to them. With love and understanding, the Church reaches out to all God's children, including [those with same-sex attraction].'"[1] My attractions to men are a complex reality for me. Instead of choosing to be gay, I actively chose to be straight for years. And yet, when prayer and fasting and dating and temple worship and service and therapy didn't alter my attractions even a little, I started to wonder if maybe I was meant to be this way. And that was very unsettling.

---

1 M. Russell Ballard, "Be Still, and Know That I Am God," CES devotional, May 4, 2014; quoting "Love One Another: A Discussion on Same-Sex Attraction," from the former mormonsandgays.org.

THAT YOUR BURDENS MAY BE LIGHT

Why did you come out?

Someone has said that people would rather be understood than be loved. In truth, the surest way to increase our love for someone is to listen with patience and respect. I believe that our baptismal covenant demands this. How can we "mourn with those that mourn" and "bear one another's burdens" (Mosiah 18:8–9) if we don't listen to know what those burdens are?

–VIRGINIA HINCKLEY PEARCE, "Ward and Branch Families:
Part of Heavenly Father's Plan for Us," *Ensign*, Nov. 1993

As I did my best to be straight, I fell into the same pattern again and again. I'd meet a great woman and see some potential in a romantic relationship. We would go out on dates, I'd enjoy our friendship, but I'd never have any desire to hold hands or kiss or show physical affection. The more this pattern played out, the more worried I became. I'd been home from my mission for more than two years, and I couldn't ignore what had gone wrong with these relationships. My lack of attraction to these attractive women was the problem. My orientation towards men and lack of orientation towards women rose to the front of my mind, and so did feelings of depression. I began to withdraw from people in my life and started to isolate myself. A good deal of my socializing had been motivated by dating and my hope for marriage. As that began to fade, so did my social interactions, and my social circle shifted dramatically. This happened at the same time that many friends from my ward moved out. I remember standing at my kitchen window, looking at the apartment building across the courtyard, and realizing I didn't know most of the new people in those apartments. And I didn't have the energy to get to know them either.

During this time, some friends invited me to go to a movie with them. As we sat in the theater waiting for the movie to start, one of them asked, "Are you doing all right, Ben? You haven't seemed like yourself lately."

In the few seconds I paused before responding, my brain raced through all the implications of this question. This friend had noticed my behavior change, and she legitimately cared about me, but how could I tell her what was going on, especially in a movie theater? In my heart I said, *If you knew what was really going on, you would hate me.* Instead I said, "No, I'm fine." I was terrified and unprepared for the rejection I was sure would follow. I still held on to the hope that no one would ever have to know how I truly felt.

I started to listen very intently to anything that was said at church about same-sex attraction, hoping to find some guidance. One Church leader explained that these attractions aren't something that people like me would be stuck with forever. Same-sex attraction did not exist in the pre-earth life, he said, and it wouldn't exist in the next. But for some unknown reason, these feelings were part of some people's mortal experience. When I first heard this, I was so relieved. I wanted to get rid of my attractions so much, and it was comforting to know that they had an expiration date. I was relieved that I never had to tell anyone about this. I just had to white-knuckle through life, keep my secret, and it would all go away with my death.

Understanding that my same-sex attraction was a mortal condition made me wish I had a terminal illness. I had prayed and prayed to be straight, but God didn't give me that answer. Church leaders used words like *affliction, temptation, inclination,* and *struggle* to describe experiences like mine. I longed for the day when God would take me home so that I could be free of all this. I would've rather been dead and straight than alive and gay. Being taught that this was an affliction and struggle of this life was comforting at first, but then it just made me wish I could pass on to the next. That promised time of rest couldn't come fast enough. This poem by Carol Lynn Pearson perfectly describes how this time felt: "I dim / I dim / I have no doubt / If someone blew I would go out." Eventually I came to learn that the next stanza describes me too: "I did not. / I must be brighter / than I thought."[1]

A friend from my ward stopped by my apartment one night and announced to me and my three roommates that a classmate of hers had just come out to her at dinner. She came over because she didn't know what to do. My ears perked up because up to that point, I had thought I was the only gay student at BYU. It hadn't even occurred to me that there could be others. I was intensely interested in what she had to say, but I had to do a delicate dance of not seeming too interested while also getting information from her. I didn't want to arouse suspicion that I might be gay.

One of the things she had learned from her friend was that there were gay BYU students who wrote anonymous blogs about their experiences. As soon as she left, I went to my room and Googled "gay byu student blog." I immediately found about a

---

1 Carol Lynn Pearson, *Goodbye, I Love You* (Springville, UT: Cedar Fort), 1990.

dozen of them. At first it was so healing to know that there were other people at my university going through what I was going through. Even though I didn't know their names and only knew them by their pseudonyms, I felt less alone. Many of the blogs had dozens of posts, and I spent hours devouring their stories. So much of what they said resonated with me. Almost all of them started the same way. They explained that they were Latter-day Saints who experienced same-sex attraction and that they were going to stay true to their covenants. I was walking the same path with the same commitment. Then as months and sometimes years passed, most of them ended up in same-sex relationships and outside of the Church. I started to wonder if that's what would happen to me, too. Was that going to be the end of my story? If we're walking the same path, is that where my path is leading, too?

One night I was reading a blog post alone in my room, feeling really trapped. I'd pushed aside my feelings for so long, and I finally let my mind wander down the two paths I thought I could take. I began to allow myself to see my life as it was. If I stayed in the Church, I would be single, lonely, and sad for the rest of my life. That felt like a path that was too hard to take. Yet if I left the Church and pursued a same-sex relationship, I'd have to leave behind this gospel and these teachings that I love. That path seemed too difficult as well. At the time, these seemed like the only two choices available to me, and they both seemed unbearable.

That night I felt compelled to get on my knees and open my heart up to my Heavenly Father. I told Him that if He needed me to be lonely and sad for the next sixty years, I was willing to do that to show Him how faithful I could be. I got up from my knees not feeling any better. I grabbed my scriptures and randomly opened them up to Alma 40:8. There's a line in that verse that says, "And time only is measured unto men." I thought, *Well, I just told God that I'm willing to be lonely and sad for the next sixty years*, and He just told me, "That's not that long." I thought that was my answer—that God was asking me to sacrifice my desire for companionship.

Talking to God had been good for me. There was no value in hiding my feelings from my Creator, since He already knew who I was. It had also been good for me to be let into the lives of those anonymous bloggers, to see people who had similar life experiences. I had so many thoughts to write down and explore, but I couldn't put them in my journal, because someday I might have kids who would read it and know that I was gay. So I kept a secret journal for my biggest secret. There are only eleven entries in it, and they are filled with fear, hope, and the most honest things I'd ever written. Part of my first entry on June 27, 2007, says, "Since I was a teenager I have struggled with same-gender attraction. This is the first time I've ever admitted that fact except in prayer." I was twenty-three years old. Admitting that on paper was a big deal because admitting it made it real. I went on to say how afraid I was of leaving the Church.

I wrote openly for the first time. These written words allowed me to see what was transpiring in my own head and heart, letting me take a step back and really observe my own life in a way that I hadn't before. What I saw were pages and pages of fear. I feared that I would leave the Church. I feared that I would be alone forever. I feared that people would find out I was attracted to guys. On June 28, 2007, I wrote, "I'm scared that I'll have to admit my same-gender attraction to my family. I know they'd still love me and support me, but I know that it'd be hard for them to deal with. I'd rather go through this alone than hurt my parents." I knew that I could trust them, but how could I ever tell them? I wanted to protect them and thought that I was strong enough to deal with it on my own.

Throughout the journal I beg for understanding. For example, on July 7, 2007, I wrote, "What is the reason for this trial? I know that someday it will end and I pray that God will hasten the day." The next day I wrote, "I pray that God will help me know what my mission and purpose is. If it isn't to get married, then what is it?" The word *trial* appears over and over again. I tried to be as righteous and faithful as I possibly could be, but I just kept spiraling downward. Then in my journal I quoted Job 13:15: "Though he slay me, yet will I trust in him." Even though I was dying on the inside, I had to trust God.

On July 13, 2007, I wrote, "I've wanted to tell my roommate Craig about my same-sex attraction, but I don't know if that would be a good idea. Would I find a good support system or lose a friend?" These months were some of the darkest of my life—months when I just wanted to disappear because facing the future felt too hard. I resonated with Joseph Smith who, after months in Liberty Jail, cried out, "O God, where art thou? And where is the pavilion that covereth thy hiding place?" (D&C 121:1). Why wasn't God answering my prayers to end my trial? Where was He? Part of the Lord's response to Joseph's pleading was, "Thy friends do stand by thee" (v. 9). Reminding Joseph that his friends were by his side is how Heavenly Father comforted him in the moment when he cried out for help. There are only eleven entries in my secret journal because the next month I found that my friends would stand by me.

I bought a copy of the final Harry Potter book the day it came out, on July 21, 2007. Or rather, my mom bought three copies and gave one to me. The previous three months had been miserable. Diving into the world of Harry Potter had been a welcome escape from reality. Much like Harry, I felt that it was up to me, and me alone, to conquer an evil that only I could defeat. Both Harry and I failed to realize that we didn't have to do this on our own—we had friends who would fight the battle with us. I don't typically cry when I read books. I didn't cry when any of Harry's beloved friends died in the last book, but I did have a good sob at one particular part. Harry, Hermione, and Ron return to Hogwarts towards the end of the book knowing the last battle is about to happen. All the students are evacuated from the school, but all the Gryffindors and all the Hufflepuffs stay to fight with Harry. As Harry witnesses student after student pledge to remain with him, I wondered if my friends would do the same. This act of loyalty and self-sacrifice, as they collectively bore Harry's burden with him, moved me to tears. Not many days after reading about Harry's friends standing with him in his hardest moment, I finally revealed my burden to two of my friends. I learned that they were just as loyal.

Humility and vulnerability are companion principles. It takes humility, stripping one's self of pride and pretense, to truly be seen. It took humility for the Roman centurion to ask Christ to heal his servant. It took vulnerability for the woman with the issue of blood to reach out and touch Jesus in a crowd. It took humility for Zeezrom to ask Alma and Amulek for a blessing after he had publicly criticized them. It took vulnerability for the prodigal son to return and to ask to be let back into the family. In a supreme act of vulnerability, the Savior asked three of His disciples to watch with Him. He asked His closest friends to be with Him. Then He prayed three separate times, saying, "O my Father, if it be possible, let this cup pass from me: nevertheless not as I will, but as thou wilt" (Matthew 26:39). Jesus Christ was vulnerable enough to ask for a way out, but He was humble enough to do His Father's will. It's a very human thing to not want to do something difficult, but it's a Christlike attribute to do it anyway.

I tried to be humble and I tried to be vulnerable, but every time I considered coming out to a friend and letting that person into my life, I would chicken out. God, being merciful and kind, orchestrated the ideal setting for me to come out. On the evening of August 12, 2007, my friend Mitch called to see if I wanted to go on a walk. We had been best friends in high school, but in all our years of friendship neither of us had ever invited the other to go on a walk. When I got off the phone I asked my roommate Craig if he wanted to join us—also something we'd never done before. As I drove us over to Mitch's apartment, I started to get so nervous I felt physically ill. I thought I might actually throw up. The three of us ended up walking through Kiwanis Park a few blocks east of BYU. I thought that maybe I shouldn't tell them I was gay, maybe this wasn't the right time. Then I considered the circumstances that had brought me to a quiet place with two of the people I trusted most in the world, and I knew I had to tell them.

I asked if we could sit on the grass because I wanted to tell them something. I hemmed and hawed for a few minutes, not sure if I could get the words out. I slowly pulled out blades of grass because I couldn't look Mitch and Craig in the face. As I tugged on the grass and stared at the ground, I reminded myself that I had been wanting to let people in for months, that I needed to do this, and that God had put me in the best possible situation to do so. And so, I took a deep breath, and for the first time uttered the words that I had stolen from an anonymous blogger: "For as long as I can remember, I've been more attracted to men than women."

After saying out loud what I had been afraid to admit my

entire life, I looked up expectantly at Mitch and Craig to see how they would react. They both said that they were surprised and caught off-guard. Then they did exactly what I needed them to do—they said that they cared about me and that I could talk to them about what I was going through whenever I needed to. Mitch spoke the most at first while Craig was pretty quiet. I didn't know how he was experiencing this new piece of information. I looked over at him and said, "Craig, I understand if you don't want to be my roommate anymore."

He looked surprised and replied, "Why wouldn't I want to be your roommate? You're the same person you've always been."

Even though I didn't know it, that's exactly what I needed him to say. I had felt broken and unworthy, thinking that no one would like me if they knew that I experienced same-sex attraction.

Letting Mitch and Craig into my experiences was the beginning of my healing. My life changed for the better that evening. I didn't anticipate the remarkable transformation that was going to take place in my life when I began to be vulnerable with my friends. As I talked with Mitch and Craig, I felt an enormous burden being lifted off my shoulders—a burden whose immense weight I had not even realized I was carrying until it was lifted. In the Book of Mormon, Alma taught his people that when we are baptized we covenant to "bear one another's burdens, that they may be light" and "to mourn with those that mourn" and to "comfort those that stand in need of comfort" (Mosiah 18:8–9). My friends willingly shared my burden, and it did indeed become light to me. I do not think that I would be an active participant in the Church today if Mitch and Craig had not reacted by expressing love and acceptance.

The burden I thought I was carrying was same-sex attraction.

That's what I believed needed to be healed. However, the affliction I was really struggling with was shame. Shame and self-hatred weighed me down. Over the years as my courage increased, I opened up to more and more people, and that weight got lighter and lighter until the shame and self-hate were completely gone. Mitch and Craig were the beginning of that transformation. I may not have had the courage to continue on that path had my friends not listened to me, loved me, and sincerely tried to understand me. My friends were just like Hermione, who told her buddy Harry, "We're with you whatever happens."

MY HAPPILY EVER AFTER THAT
HAPPILY NEVER HAPPENED

Why don't you marry a woman?

We all search for happiness, and we all try to find our own "happily ever after." The truth is, God knows how to get there! And He has created a map for you; He knows the way.

—DIETER F. UCHTDORF, "Your Happily Ever After," *Ensign*, May 2010

"Heavenly Father," I prayed, "please help me to be attracted to women and not to men."

After hundreds of those prayers, I switched tactics. I prayed, "Heavenly Father, I can handle not acting on my attractions to guys, but please just make me bisexual and help me be attracted to women."

After hundreds of those prayers, I pleaded, "Heavenly Father, just send me one girl, one girl that I can be attracted to."

When I came out to Mitch and Craig, the words spoken aloud felt incredibly real, and I was faced with the fact that my prayers had not been answered. Marriage no longer felt possible, so I chose to accept reality and hunker down in a single life. I couldn't see any other options. At the time I was working as a Spanish teacher at the Missionary Training Center. I had a small class with just six missionaries who were struggling with their teaching. They would give the same lesson every time without taking into consideration the person they were teaching. I had a bright idea to have them all teach me the plan of salvation together so they could practice teaching a personalized lesson. "Elders, I already know the plan of salvation. I could draw all the circles and lines and teach it as well as anyone. But there is something that *you* can teach *me* about it. Teach me, as Brother Schilaty." I stepped out of the room and gave them twenty minutes to prepare.

When I came back, they taught a generic lesson as if I had never heard of the plan of salvation before. I told them that it was a good lesson, but that it wasn't personalized to me. I invited them to pray and ask God what I, Brother Schilaty, needed to know about the plan of salvation. I also explained that missionaries aren't really teaching anything new; they are reminding people of what they once knew, and there was something I needed to be reminded of. I stepped out of the room for a few minutes to give them time to plan.

The next lesson was completely different. One of the elders began, "I feel prompted to ask you why you came to BYU."

I replied, "To be honest, I came here for all the girls. It's the best place to get married."

He then asked, "And how is that going?"

"Not well," I admitted. I told them that I hadn't been on a date in months, but didn't tell them why. This gave them the direction they needed. They then taught me about the plan of salvation focusing on eternal families. One of the missionaries boldly told me that marriage was the next step in the plan for me and that I needed to be working hard to make that happen. The elders all got really personal and shared some deeply intimate experiences. Five of the six cried during the lesson as they opened up their hearts to me. At the end of the lesson they invited me to make marriage a priority. The Spirit in the room was palpable, and I committed to follow their invitation. Before this lesson I had given up on dating, but as the missionaries talked, I was prompted to do a 180 and reverse my course. The Holy Ghost impressed upon me that I needed to make dating and marriage a priority. I felt heavenly confirmation that that was the course God wanted me to take. I had seen a piece of His map for me.

After the lesson, I invited them all to take a moment to write down what they had learned from the experience. One elder said it was the first time he had taught a person and not a lesson. Another hugged me as he left class and asked, "Is that what it's like to teach by the Spirit?"

"Yes," I replied, "that's exactly what it's like." After they left, I sat in the classroom by myself for a few minutes pondering the miracle that had just occurred. The elders had said a lot of great things, but it was the Spirit that had taught me. I learned that I needed to have faith that the Lord was guiding my life. I walked out of that classroom firmly committed to making marriage a priority. Two months later, I met Emma (name has been changed).

I was traveling home from BYU to Seattle for Christmas break. Trying to get a head start on the readings for next semester, I read *Latin America: Its Problems and Its Promises* while waiting to board the plane. A tall, beautiful, blonde woman standing near me asked what boarding number I had. She was supposed to be a few people behind me, but I told her she could cut and stand with me. She asked what I was reading and I showed her my book. Our conversation then went like this:

Her: Do you speak Spanish?

Me: *Claro que sí.* I served a mission in Mexico.

Her: Awesome! I served a mission in Bolivia.

Me: No way! I lived in Bolivia last year!

That was it. We became friends that fast. In the three minutes we talked while boarding the plane, I learned that we were both BYU students and both worked at the MTC. She sat a row away from me, and when the flight attendant was taking drink orders I heard her ask for Sprite and orange juice. That sounded delicious, so I ordered the same thing. As the flight was landing, the luggage compartment door above me opened and Emma yelled, "Ben!" and pointed to it. Using my go-go-Gadget arms I closed the door. I beamed that this beautiful girl had just witnessed me being a hero. Before we got off the plane, I wondered how I could strike up a conversation with her again. She must have felt similarly, because as soon as we were in the terminal, before I could get up the nerve to approach her, she walked up to me and asked what I'd been listening to on the plane. We then bonded over our mutual love for the musical *Wicked.* As we walked through the airport I knew I wanted to get her number. I also knew that my parents would be waiting at baggage claim, and I did not want to ask her out in front of them. So, with no time to lose, I told her that I would love to take her out in a few weeks when we got back to Provo. She seemed excited and we exchanged numbers. She then met my parents.

I hadn't planned on seeing Emma until after the break, but I woke up two days later to a call from her. She wanted to hear about my internship in Bolivia and how she could do something similar. We talked for more than an hour. Emma and I immediately got along really well. We just clicked. We hung out in Washington over the break and then went on a few dates when we got back to Provo. I liked her so much. She was fun, beautiful, witty, spiritual, and just a blast to be around. I wanted to spend as much time with her as possible. She was a light in my life. After our first official date, I wrote in my journal: "Emma is such a cool girl and she is so much fun. She's pretty much perfect for me, except that I don't find her attractive. She's pretty, but I'm just not that attracted to her. Honestly, today I really wished I wasn't me. I finally find an awesome girl that's interested in me, but I still have SSA."

Wanting to be different was a common yearning for me at this time in my life. Alma cried, "O that I were an angel, and could have the wish of mine heart, that I might go forth and speak with the trump of God, with a voice to shake the earth, and cry repentance unto every people!" (Alma 29:1). I was desiring, "O that I were a straight man, and could marry a woman like I'm supposed to!" Alma's desire was a little more selfless than mine. He wanted to save the whole world by preaching repentance, and I was just trying to save myself. I wanted to live a traditional life, walk the path I'd been taught to walk, and do what God was requiring of me. It took me years to learn the lesson that Alma teaches a few verses later: "I ought to be content with the things which the Lord hath allotted unto me" (v. 3). I didn't know how to do that. I didn't know how to be content with the circumstances that God had placed me in.

One week after our first date, Emma became the seventh person I came out to. We had a double date planned with two of my friends later that week, and they both knew I was gay. I didn't think it would be fair for Emma to be the only person on the date to not know that I was attracted to men. That sense of obligation gave me the courage to tell her, even though we'd known each other for less than a month. I picked her up at her apartment when I got off work. I didn't know where to go. I couldn't talk to her in my apartment because I didn't want my roommates to overhear us, and we couldn't stay in her apartment because I for sure didn't want her roommates to know. It was also much too cold to go on a walk. So she got in my car and I made the extremely cheesy decision to drive to the Provo temple parking lot. With the temple glowing in front of us, I told her that I had SSA, which was how I described my orientation when I was twenty-three. Her initial reaction was, "That sucks." She asked me if I thought I'd ever get married, and I said I wasn't sure. I told her that I'd like to give us a try, but that I'd like to move slowly. She wanted to give us a try, too.

A few days later I wrote: "Emma really wants to date me, but she's worried that she might get hurt. I worry about that too because I don't want to hurt her, but I also want to try. What if this is my chance?" I just couldn't believe that someone as wonderful and cool as her who knew that I was attracted to guys was willing to date me. I felt like an unlovable beast, and somehow Belle had come into my life and loved me anyway. Emma would be my fairy-tale ending. I wrote a few days later: "She's a miracle." My journal is riddled with entries where I say, "I love Emma, but . . ." and "Emma is so perfect for me, but . . ." and "I'm so lucky to have Emma in my life, but . . ." and "I have such a blast with Emma, but . . ." I tried to be so open and honest with her. I wanted her to know how wonderful and beautiful she was, but I also needed her to know that I wasn't really attracted to her. I needed her to know what she was getting herself into.

I had to hold her hand. That's what boyfriends do. But there was nothing inside of me compelling me to. One evening on a walk I asked if I could hold her hand and she said, "No, because you don't want to." I convinced her that I did, and she let me. I felt uncomfortable. We held hands while watching a movie that night and I was trying to let it feel natural. We didn't hold hands again for another week. On my birthday, Emma planned this really nice dinner for me and a "surprise" party that I knew about. We watched a movie after with some friends, and she and I started holding hands at the beginning of the movie. Not long into the movie I pretended that I needed to go to the bathroom so that I would have an excuse to let go of her hand. When I sat back down, I didn't hold her hand again for the rest of the movie. I was stuck. Not holding her hand made me feel bad because I knew I was supposed to. But holding her hand made me feel bad because it made me uncomfortable.

More than a month passed and I still hadn't kissed her. I'd never kissed anyone and neither had she, and she was beginning to get understandably impatient. I knew I was supposed to kiss her, but I just couldn't get up the courage to do it. A friend confided in me that he had so much trouble *not* kissing a woman on the first date. I couldn't believe how different our worlds were. One night, Emma and I went to a BYU men's volleyball game together and I thought it would be such a great story if I kissed her in the bleachers while we were watching the game. I imagined quickly stealing a kiss and then the whole crowd would cheer and it'd be awesome. She'd love my assertiveness and it'd be a great story to tell our kids, but I just couldn't do it. Probably better that I didn't.

I took her home after the game and went back to my apartment feeling so mad at myself for not being able to kiss her. I stewed for a few minutes, decided I wasn't going to let fear control me, grabbed my backpack, and went back to her house. She was surprised and happy to see me. The two of us sat on her couch together and studied for a bit. We also talked about kissing and what it meant. She assured me that it wasn't a big deal, attempting to take some of the pressure off. I knew that I needed to stop being afraid and that I couldn't leave without kissing her. When I stood up to leave she stood up as well, and we shared a brief, tender, incredibly chaste kiss. As I pulled away, I looked into her eyes and smiled. I then turned around away from her to grab my backpack, and the smile vanished from my face. With my head turned from her I let my real emotions show on my face. I started shaking as I grabbed my backpack. As I turned to face her, I put a fake smile back on my face and tried to control the shaking so she wouldn't notice the discomfort I was feeling. I gave her a hug and left her house.

As soon as the door shut I started running to my car. As I ran, I said to myself out loud, "What have I done? What have I done? What have I done?" I sat in my car feeling like garbage. I felt like I had just lied to her, that I had expressed something that I didn't really feel. When I got home I told my roommates I had kissed her. They were all excited, and I feigned excitement as well. The next day I was back at Emma's house talking to her roommates before she got home. They told me that they had heard all about the kiss and how magical it was from Emma. They were so giddy about it, but the thought that kept running through my mind was, *She and I did not experience the same thing.*

I kissed Emma a few more times hoping I'd like it more, but I didn't. I even took her to the exact spot where I had come out to Mitch and Craig. I kissed her there and in my head said, *Haha! Take that, same-sex attraction!* Not long after our first kiss I got the flu and was grateful I had an excuse to not kiss her. And then not long after that she broke up with me. I was pretty upset and very hurt. I couldn't understand how the relationship had ended. I had met her right after feeling prompted to start dating again, and it felt like we were meant to get married. She was my chance. It couldn't be over. But not only that, I loved having her in my life, and losing that relationship was painful. I had told her I loved her and that was true, but one of my first thoughts after she dumped me was to hope that she'd be single for a long time so she'd regret breaking up with me. When you love someone, you don't hope that they'll be filled with regret, but that's what I hoped for. At the time I didn't realize how selfish I was being.

Loving a woman as a gay man is complicated. A month after Emma broke up with me, I moved to Mexico for a summer internship. During the trip my hair gel exploded in my bag, covering my journal and rendering some other books in my bag unsalvageable. When I saw my journal covered in goo my first thought was, *Oh no! Emma!* All of my memories of her were written in that book, and I was terrified of losing the record of a relationship that had meant so much to me. I was so relieved when I realized that, though damaged, the journal was still readable. I missed her terribly. I missed having her in my life. She had become my best friend. However, the relationship was problematic, because I loved spending time with her, but the pressure to show physical affection made me so uncomfortable.

As years passed and I matured, I learned that if I really care for someone I'll want what's best for that person. And I wasn't the best thing for Emma. She deserved someone who could love her in ways that I couldn't, someone who could be more than just a great friend. When she did get married, I didn't feel an ounce of jealousy, hurt, or regret. All I felt was happiness for my friend and her happiness—that she was moving towards her happily ever after. I was glad that she dumped me because, as much as I had originally wished and thought it, we were not each other's happily ever after. "Charity . . . seeketh not her own" (1 Corinthians 13:4–5). I loved Emma, I really did. But I lacked charity. Much of our relationship was about me and how it was supposed to complete *me* and make *me* happy and save *me* from my life of loneliness and shame. When she dumped me, I thought about myself and how I was hurt. Her feelings were secondary to mine. I had a lot to learn.

A few months after Emma and I broke up, I was watching a movie and really missing her. An inspired thought came to my mind: "If you love her, you will let her go." Then as I thought more, I realized that she was never mine to begin with. She didn't need me to let her go. I needed to let go of this relationship that wasn't going to work. I wanted to hold on to this relationship that had been so good for me in a lot of ways, a relationship that was supposed to fix all of my problems. But that wasn't fair to either of us. I know I sound like a broken record, but this was my reality. For months I was trying to figure out how to keep this relationship that wasn't working for either of us, because I didn't know how else to move forward.

Sister Michelle Craig pointed out that Moses, Nephi, and the brother of Jared were all commanded to cross large bodies of water, but they each were led to do so in different ways. They received "personalized direction, tailored to them, and each trusted and acted. The Lord is mindful of those who obey and, in the words of Nephi, will 'prepare a way for [us to] accomplish the thing which he commandeth.' Note that Nephi says, 'a way'— not 'the way'" ("Spiritual Capacity," *Ensign*, Nov. 2019). I had felt that there was one way to do life right, and that meant being married to a woman. Emma and I were each other's first kiss, which led me to believe that our relationship was meant to be. I was stuck believing that she was *the* way to do God's will for me. I hadn't yet understood what Sister Craig taught, that the Lord can use many means to bring us to the promised land. Emma was part of my map, but not my destination.

I can't say enough nice things about Emma. She is kind, witty, smart, accomplished, and legitimately made me a better person. We haven't spoken face to face since 2012, but her in-fluence in my life is incalculable. In 2014, months before I had any intention of coming out publicly, I sent her an essay I had written that later became my coming-out post. Her response was to quote Esther 4:14: "For if thou altogether holdest thy peace at this time, then shall there enlargement and deliverance arise to the Jews from another place; but thou and thy father's house shall be destroyed: and who knoweth whether thou art come to the kingdom for such a time as this?" That scripture hit me like a ton of bricks, and it stirred in me a desire to speak, to no longer hold my peace. Emma unknowingly inspired me with part of the courage I needed to be more vocal. I thank God for Emma's pres-ence in my life.

I often get asked by other LGBTQ Latter-day Saints if they should marry someone of the opposite sex. I really don't know what anyone else should do. My friend Sarah self-identifies as bisexual and she is married to a gay man. When people ask her why she married a gay man, she responds simply, "Because we fell in love." Sarah's answer is beautiful. Had I married Emma, my answer to that question would not have been the same. I was in a place where I might have married a woman because there was an expectation to do so, to fulfill a societal role. That would have been a disaster.

People also ask me why I don't just marry a woman that I'm good friends with, since marriage is about so much more than sex. I can't really speak to what marriage is like, having never been married, but I agree that marriage is about so much more than sex. I try to imagine what it would be like to be this hypothetical wife. I wonder what it would be like to be married to someone that I knew wasn't attracted to me. I wonder what it would be like to be married to someone who didn't want to hold my hand.

I wonder what it would be like to be married to someone who didn't want to kiss me or cuddle with me. I think that would be really hard on me. And that is the position that I was putting Emma in.

In recent years I've started to say "orientation" more than "sexual orientation." Yes, I am sexually attracted to men and not to women, but it's about so much more than that. I'm also emotionally oriented towards men, and romantically oriented towards men, and intellectually orientated towards men, and even spiritually orientated towards men. All the parts of me that yearn for connection are directed towards men. And I don't feel that same orientation towards women. I think I'd make a great husband, but man, it would be hard if I weren't physically, emotionally, romantically, intellectually, or spiritually attracted to my wife. Hard for me, but perhaps even harder for her if she were physically, emotionally, romantically, intellectually, and spiritually attracted to me and knew that those feelings were not reciprocated.

I have pondered why I felt the Spirit tell me to pursue a heterosexual marriage during that lesson with the missionaries when I was twenty-three. I believe that I needed to go down that path to learn that it wasn't for me. I don't believe that the Spirit was inspiring me to marry a woman, but that He was inspiring me to *pursue* marriage to a woman. There is a difference here. You see, when I came out, I not only gave up trying to get married, but I lost a lot of hope for the future. I thought that I was resigned to a life of sadness and I just needed to hunker down and white-knuckle my way through life until I died. That was not the kind of life God wanted me to live. And so, God spoke to me as the missionaries were teaching me so that I could begin to have hope in the future again. Feeling inspired to pursue marriage led me to build a life that is turning out to be quite beautiful, even though I'm still single. Right now my life is just me. I'm the only person I need to take care of. But I don't know what the future holds. I want to be prepared for any future that God has prepared for me, and that might include a future in which other people are in my care.

Life is about growth and working to become like the Savior. Sister Craig taught, "As His faithful disciple, you can receive personal inspiration and revelation, consistent with His commandments, that is tailored to you. You have unique missions and roles to perform in life and will be given unique guidance to fulfill them" ("Spiritual Capacity," *Ensign*, Nov. 2019). God led Emma and me to each other. My relationship with her taught me to love in a charitable way, and that was a beautiful gift. My life would be poorer had I not followed the prompting to pursue marriage to a woman. Sometimes Heavenly Father leads us to relationships that won't be permanent because He needs two of His children to learn things from each other. And in learning those things, they'll each be led to their own happily ever afters.

RELATIONSHIPS FOR ETERNITY

Why do you stay in the Church?

You see, the names "brother" and "sister" are not just friendly greetings or terms of endearment for us. They are an expression of an eternal truth: God is the literal Father of all mankind; we are each part of His eternal family.

–HENRY B. EYRING, "Gathering the Family of God," *Ensign,* May 2017

I left BYU with a bachelor's degree in hand in 2008 at the age of twenty-four. Over the next four years I would move back to Washington to teach middle school and high school Spanish and return to BYU for a master's degree. During those years I came out to close friends and some family, but my orientation was far from the focal point of my life. I still dated women because I believed that I would get married someday. Not because of any spiritual prompting, but because I felt that I had no other choice. Marrying a woman was the only real option that I saw. In August of 2012 I moved to Tucson, Arizona, to start a PhD program.

Before I moved to Tucson there was one thing that I prayed for fervently. With my parents and siblings more than a thousand miles away, I prayed that God would send me a second family. I got to Tucson on a Saturday night and was a stranger to the residents of my new town. I arrived at my new house and met my roommate, Kevin Minch. The next day he invited me over to his parents' house for Sunday dinner, and I gladly accepted. Kevin's family knew nothing about me except that I was new to town and far from home. They took me into their home just as true followers of Jesus Christ would have. "For I was an hungred, and ye gave me meat: I was thirsty, and ye gave me drink: I was a stranger, and ye took me in" (Matthew 25:35). They continued inviting me over for Sunday dinners, and I became part of the family. I refer to Kevin's family as "my Tucson family," and his parents have referred to me as their third son.

I was twenty-eight when I moved to Tucson, and thirty was quickly approaching. I felt like I was running out of time to get married. My friend Allison came to Tucson during her winter break to visit some relatives and wanted to hang out with me while she was in town. She and I had been good friends at BYU, she knew I was gay, and I knew she had a crush on me. Before she visited, I wondered if maybe, just maybe, we could date. Allison is super rad, very pretty, and absolutely hilarious. Who better to marry than her? But when we hung out, I felt absolutely no physical connection and I scrapped the idea pretty quickly. She did, however, meet my roommate Kevin. Allison thought Kevin was pretty cool, and Kevin thought Allison was pretty neat. I worked my magic and helped them set up a Skype date after Allison returned home. They then fell in love and got married.

A few weeks into their long-distance dating, Kevin asked me why Allison and I had never dated. I dodged the question, but he continued to press the issue. I wasn't quite ready to come out to Kevin because I had no idea what he thought about LGBTQ stuff. Saying that "I just never thought of her like that" wasn't satisfying to him, so I finally told him that I was gay. The conversation unfolded while I was folding laundry. I was grateful to have something to do with my hands, because I didn't want to look him in the eyes. I could tell from the look on his face that this was not the reason he was expecting. But Kevin is one of the finest men I know, and he spent a lot of time listening to me and trying to understand me in the months that followed.

Since I was close to both Kevin and Allison, I heard about their relationship regularly. And because of our paper-thin doors, I could hear them Skyping and falling in love every night. I was mostly happy for them, but I was also sad for me. I wrote the following in my journal: "I kind of snapped at Kevin last night. He kept talking to me about Allison and how happy he was and I was just feeling crappy. His happiness just made me feel worse. I went to bed feeling pretty sorry for myself. I felt like Eliza from *My Fair Lady* when she exclaimed, 'What's to become of me?'" Here I was, now twenty-nine years old, and two of my best friends were about to abandon me for each other. I envisioned a future in which I would constantly be left behind as others moved on. Always alone and always on my own.

A week before Allison and Kevin got married, I went to Kevin's bachelor party. It was less bachelor party and more just dinner with Kevin's cousins and a few friends. I realized as we talked about the upcoming wedding that Kevin was incredibly excited for everything about being married to Allison. I put myself in his shoes and wondered how I would be feeling if I were about to get married. The idea of physical intimacy petrified me, but Kevin was looking forward to it. I realized, more than ever, that I never could have married Allison. Talented, beautiful, wonderful, hilarious, accomplished Allison who had liked me for years was someone I just couldn't have an intimate relationship with. She was marrying my friend, and I was so glad she was marrying him and not me. If I couldn't fall in love with Allison, then who could

I fall in love with? Up to this point I had remained confident that I'd find a woman I could marry, but now I wasn't so sure.

I found myself reading the words of Nephi and fixating on his description of being led by fear. He said that he "shrunk." As someone who very much likes being tall, I found the idea of shrinking especially unappealing. I reflected on my dating past and realized just how much of it had been driven by fear of being alone. And not only that, but feeling that dating was a requirement, something that God was compelling me to do. Then I read in 2 Nephi 2:14 that there are "things to act and things to be acted upon." I was nearly toppled over by the realization that God would not force me to do anything, that it was my choice. I envisioned my future self, coming home every day to one of the women I had previously dated. I really tried to feel and experience what that life would be like. And I realized that that wasn't what I wanted. As I did this mental exercise, I felt the fear I had experienced for years melt away. I felt the comforting presence of the Holy Ghost teaching me that Heavenly Father would not force me down any path, and that He would honor my agency. I prayed for continued courage and, devoid of fear for the first time, made the choice to stop dating women.

Right before the wedding, I moved across town and into a new singles ward. There was a guy in the ward I had talked to a few times, and I had a big crush on him. When I got home from church one Sunday, I was thinking about how much I liked this guy, and then I thought about how desperately I had wanted to like Allison and just couldn't. The experience of liking this guy at church felt so different from trying to like Allison. I had a crush on a guy, and the fact that I could never date him (or any other guy, for that matter) was painful and frustrating. I began to wonder if maybe I was doing life all wrong. I'd been reading a lot of stories online about gay

Latter-day Saints and listening to a lot of podcast interviews as well. It seemed like almost every gay Latter-day Saint man either married a woman or left the Church (and they often ended up doing both). I'd spent the last eight years trying to marry a woman and had never really had a serious girlfriend. Perhaps it was time to date someone I actually wanted to date. I'd been making one choice for eight years with no success, so I figured it was time to try something new.

At this point I hadn't missed church once in eleven years, and I decided it was time to end the streak and take a break. Almost no one in my new ward knew me, so I wouldn't be missed if I didn't attend. My family lived far away, and they wouldn't even have to know I wasn't going to church. It seemed like the perfect time to step away. No one would even know I was gone. I decided that I wouldn't leave for good; I'd just take a sabbatical and see if I could be happier away from the Church. If I was no longer going to date women, it was time to date men. And it felt like the companion to that choice was taking a break from church.

Six days after making this decision, I was up in Mesa for Kevin and Allison's wedding. I walked into the Mesa Arizona Temple thinking that I probably wouldn't be back within those walls for quite some time, knowing the decision I was about to make. Then during the sealing something life-changing happened. Here I was, sitting in a sealing room, surrounded by people who felt like family. It's hard to describe very spiritual experiences, but this is more or less what happened: As I watched two of my best friends kneel at an altar and make sacred covenants with each other and with God, it felt like the veil parted and we were all in heaven together—actually in heaven. I had a powerful feeling that this was all real. The promises they were making and receiving were real. The priesthood power that was sealing them was real. The potential to be together forever was real. The whole restored gospel felt real and tangible, and I didn't want to give it up. I was in a sacred place with people that I loved, and it felt like home. The best way to articulate what I felt is this: "Whatever happens, I need to be able to be with these people in this place forever." The Holy Ghost communicated to me the path I should take by reminding me of the relationships I already had that were meant to be eternal.

No one at the wedding knew that I'd been considering taking a break from church. After the sealing, I was feeling pretty overwhelmed. Not only was I extremely happy for Allison and Kevin, but I had just been reminded that the path I should choose was the one that would allow me to be in the temple and continue to build these relationships. Filled with love for my friends and new clarity about life, I hugged Kevin and Allison and told them how much I loved them. It took all the manly testosterone I could muster to keep myself from bursting into a weepy mess because I was feeling so much love and peace. I walked out of the temple, posed for pictures, and didn't tell anyone that day what I had experienced.

Like Joseph Smith and Oliver Cowdery, I had had an experience in the temple in which the "veil was taken from [my mind], and the eyes of [my] understanding were opened (D&C 110:1). I didn't see the Savior or heavenly messengers as they had, but I did have an experience with the Divine in the house of God. The message from the Holy Ghost to me had been, "Stand ye in holy places, and be not moved" (D&C 87:8). I felt called to strengthen and deepen the relationships that I had been taught would be eternal. That day in the temple, the Lord opened up my mind and showed me that the path I had chosen to take was not the path He wanted for me. Being in a sacred place opened up a conduit for God to teach me. Nephi "did go unto the mount oft" and "the Lord showed unto [him] great things" (1 Nephi 18:3). God showed me some great things, and I felt peace.

I used to talk about how I planned to "stay in the Church." That phrase made me feel like I was trapped and stagnant because I wasn't able to pursue the kind of relationship I wanted. In recent years I have started to say that I plan to "move forward in the Church." I shifted my perspective from simply staying in an organization to seeing how I can grow and thrive within the organization. Instead of looking at the ways that I have felt held back, I see the ways that I am empowered and inspired. The words of President Hugh B. Brown ring true to me today: "Now some of you as you go forward are going to meet with disappointment—perhaps many disappointments, some of them crucial. Sometimes you will wonder if God has forgotten you. Sometimes you may even wonder if He lives and where He has gone. But in these times when so many are saying God is dead and when so many are denying His existence, I think I could not leave with you a better message than this: God is aware of you individually. He knows who you are and what you are, and, furthermore, He knows what you are capable of becoming. Be not discouraged, then, if you do not get all the things you want just when you want them. Have the courage to go on and face your life and, if necessary, reverse it to bring it into harmony with His law."[1]

I had been on the brink of stepping away from the Church to pursue a life that I thought would be better for me. After making that decision, God reached out and invited me to move forward within the Church. Being in a sacred place at a significant moment allowed me to experience what really mattered to me. My relationships with friends who feel like family allowed me to be honest and open while also feeling loved and seen. Sacred places combined with special relationships permitted heaven to speak to me.

---

1 Hugh B. Brown, "God Is the Gardener" (Brigham Young University devotional, May 31, 1968), speeches.byu.edu.

Even after having this powerful, spiritual experience in the temple, my circumstances didn't change. I still felt stuck and wondered how I was supposed to make life work. A few months after the wedding, I was having a really tough day and felt like I needed a father's blessing, but my dad was 1,600 miles away. Kevin's dad, Ken, was the closest thing I had to a father in Tucson, so I texted him and asked if he could give me a blessing, which he was happy to do. He listened to me as I unloaded all my problems onto him and then gave me a beautiful blessing. I hugged him afterward, and through tears I thanked him and his family for always being there for me. I left the house and cried on the way home. Not because I was sad, but because I was so incredibly grateful. I felt so grateful to have been welcomed into Kevin's family. I was grateful to always have a place to eat Sunday dinner, to never have to wonder if someone would make me a birthday cake, and to know that even though I didn't have my parents and siblings there, I was cared for and watched over by people who had become my family.

Three years after I met Kevin, I drove to the hospital to meet his and Allison's first child. In the hospital room, Kevin and Allison told me that they had chosen to give the baby my first name as his middle name. What an unexpected honor. The hospital staff had attached a card to his bassinet that said, "I'm a boy!" with all of his information on it, but Kevin and Allison had left the name space blank. They handed me the card and had me write his name on it. I had played an integral part in the creation of this new little family, and they wanted me to know that I would always be a part of it. God didn't give me the kind of family I thought I wanted, but He gave me the family I needed. And through His Spirit and my friends, He had invited me to move forward as part of my Church family.

REALLY SUPER AWESOME BEST FRIENDS

Have you acted on your feelings?

*Let us follow the Savior's path and increase our
compassion, diminish our tendency to judge, and stop
being the inspectors of the spirituality of others.*
–REYNA I. ABURTO, "Thru Cloud and Sunshine,
Lord, Abide with Me!" *Ensign,* Nov. 2019

This chapter may not be easy for some of you to read. I know that the idea of two men falling in love can make some people feel uncomfortable. I mean, it used to make me feel uncomfortable. I invite you to reflect on the experiences you have had with crushes, love, and physical affection in your life. How did you know you liked someone? How did it feel? What led you to want to kiss someone you loved? If you will take a moment to reflect on your own experiences, I think it might help you relate to mine. And maybe this particular walk in my shoes can help you see what it's like to be me.

"It's okay to be gay," I'm often told, "as long as you don't act on it." This communicates to me that it's fine to "be gay" as long as I don't "do gay things." I understood that "acting on it" included far more than behaviors that violated the law of chastity, including things that heterosexual couples were allowed to act on.

I was terrified that any little thing I did could be defined as "acting on it" and would disqualify me from being righteous. "Acting on it" was a firm line, and if I crossed that line, I'd be out.

I didn't plan to fall in love with a man, but that's what happened. I met Jordan through my brother and sister-in-law about a year after moving to Tucson. He was living in Utah and I was living in Arizona. We had met a few times in person when I was visiting family, but we didn't know each other very well. He texted me the day after Thanksgiving and I was polite but didn't really push the conversation forward. A month later, around Christmastime, I was visiting my family in Washington and he reached out again. This time we kept talking. We texted throughout the day for a few days. I had a hunch he was gay, and he was pretty sure I was gay, but at this point neither of us had acknowledged this. In my journal I wrote: "I don't want to have a crush on him, I just want to be his friend." I was both worried and flattered that Jordan would like me. On New Year's Eve we were texting about our resolutions and we started to share candid statements about ourselves. The last thing Jordan texted me that night was, "Last candid statement; I love you, Ben." I pulled out my journal and wrote: "I'm sure he meant it in the brotherly love sort of way, but it was still surprising. And it made me feel really good inside."

I sent Jordan an essay I had written about being gay. He was one of the first people to read it. My heart pounded in the minutes after pushing send. A few minutes later he texted "I am, too." We started talking on the phone regularly. We would talk about church stuff, our families, reconciling our faith with our orientation, and we laughed a lot. He is one of the cleverest, wittiest, handsomest people I have ever met. Few things are as attractive to me as a good sense of humor. My journal is riddled with entries about how happy I was to have Jordan in my life. I'd had girl-friends before that I had really connected with, but this felt different. It felt so natural and effortless. "I just feel really good about my life right now. I feel more complete with Jordan in it. I feel like he's giving me something that was missing. I reminded him tonight that we can only be friends. I think that bums him out, but he said that's okay because life with Ben in it is better than life without Ben in it."

A number of times Jordan asked me if I would be his boy-friend. I always told him no, that we couldn't do that. But we could be best friends and always be in each other's lives. As we spent more and more time together on the phone and on Skype, best friends didn't feel like a strong enough term. I told Jordan that while we couldn't date and be boyfriends, we could be really super awesome best friends. That wasn't enough for him. He wanted a real partner.

One evening Jordan got really honest. He told me that he wasn't sure that he could stay in the Church. I distinctly remember lying on my bed holding my phone to my ear, staring up at the ceiling while we talked. I told him that I just wanted him to be happy, whichever path he chose; that I'd support him in whatever decision he made. I was surprised by how emotional I got when I said, "I love you, Jordan," because I felt it so deeply. It wasn't an infatuation kind of love, but the kind of love that made me want the very, very best for him. The kind of love that wasn't about me, but was about him. And this love felt so different from the love I had felt for Emma and the other women I had dated. The love I had felt for them was more of a logical, mental love. This love for Jordan felt like it came from my soul. I wiped away tears and we kept talking. I had fallen in love with this wonderful person that I wasn't supposed to love in this way.

I didn't see this happening at the time, but as Jordan was drifting away from the Church, he was trying to bring me with him. At the same time, I remained committed to the Church and was trying to keep him from leaving. We were trying to stay together and at the same time pulling in two different directions. I lived in this black-and-white mindset of having to be either 100% in or 100% out, that if I allowed Jordan to be my boyfriend that I was automatically out of the Church.

After four months of us talking nearly every day, I traveled to Utah for work and spent a few days with Jordan. Our exclusively long-distance relationship was suddenly in person. I hadn't seen him with my own eyes for almost a year. When we hugged at the airport he said that he had forgotten how tall I was, and I noticed that he had put on too much cologne. Before the trip I had made some clear, explicit rules about what we could and couldn't do. That included no hand-holding and no kissing. After we got on the freeway he asked if he could hold my hand. I told him no and he seemed disappointed, but he respected my choice. As we drove, I thought of all the times I'd tried to hold hands with women and the few times I actually had. It had always been something I was supposed to do, not something that I wanted to do. It was a duty, and it felt uncomfortable. Now here I was sitting next to someone whose hand I desperately wanted to hold, and I was politely declining. I wondered what it would be like to hold hands with someone that I was so completely drawn to. So I made a choice. Ten minutes after saying no, I held Jordan's hand.

That night I pulled out my journal and addressed the future reader. I felt the need to explain to whoever read the account of my life why I did what I had done. I wrote: "Whoever reads this (if anyone ever does), I want them to know that I love Jordan. He is a wonderful man and he makes me so happy. I loved the feeling of being near him and holding him close to me. It felt so good and it felt like home. Cuddling with girls has always felt a little forced, but with Jordan it just felt so natural and easy. That said, I love the gospel of Jesus Christ more than anything and I will be faithful to it. I don't think there is any sin in loving Jordan and being affectionate with him. I do feel that kissing isn't a good idea and so I'll not do that, but I feel great just loving him and that's what I'll do." Despite those feelings I had a more pressing priority. I ended that journal entry saying, "Come what may, I want to do God's will."

Two nights later we kissed. I was too embarrassed to write about it in my journal because I had declared on its pages that I wouldn't. I have kissed two people in my entire life—one woman and one man. Kissing a man felt so different from kissing a woman. Instead of feeling obligated to do something that felt uncomfortable, this felt so comfortable and natural. Kissing Jordan felt on some level like what I imagine Eve must have felt when she partook of the fruit of the tree of knowledge of good and evil. My innocence was replaced with experience. Previously, when I saw people kiss in movies, I just didn't get it. When I saw romantic reunions at the airport and people would kiss, I didn't get that either. This thing that humans do made no sense to me, because I never wanted to kiss a woman. But when I kissed Jordan, suddenly everything made sense. I understood why someone would want to kiss a person they loved and why it was such a meaningful act.

The prophet Lehi taught that God placed the tree of knowledge of good and evil and the tree of life in the Garden of Eden to be in opposition to each other. He explained that "man could not act for himself save it should be that he was enticed by the one or the other" (2 Nephi 2:16). Agency cannot exist without choice.

Up until that point, I hadn't really known what I would be giving up by choosing to remain single. I knew that being affectionate with women didn't feel natural to me and that there was something very important missing in each relationship I tried to pursue. But I didn't know what deep romantic connection felt like until that moment. When Jordan and I kissed, I was given knowledge that I hadn't previously possessed. That opened my eyes and my heart to a taste of what human intimacy was all about. With my eyes opened, the implications of my choices became clear in a completely new way. Like Mother Eve, I had gained knowledge.

It was late at night when we first kissed. Jordan went to bed right after, and I sat in the guest bedroom riddled with guilt. I had gone back on a decision that I had made to not kiss him. I felt like a hypocrite. There was comfort in being able to say that I had never "acted on it" before, and now I couldn't say that. I felt like I had done something irreparable—something that I couldn't take back. It wasn't until the next morning when Jordan and I talked that I felt better. The truth was that I had wanted to kiss him. I had wanted to express physical affection. I had wanted to be in a committed romantic relationship with him. But I felt that I wasn't allowed to want those things. It was one of those rare moments when my personal desires were incongruent with what I had been taught.

When we held hands, Jordan asked me if I would be his boyfriend and I said no. Then when we kissed, he asked me again. Again I said no. "But we just kissed?" he half asked, half pleaded.

"I'm sorry," I said, "I just can't have a boyfriend." Fear led me to say this. Fear that I would do the wrong thing. Fear that I would be judged if other people found out. Fear that I would leave behind my faith. After kissing, I felt wonderful and yet incredibly conflicted. Even though I deeply wanted to be his boyfriend, I told him I couldn't. Within the span of seconds my lips did one thing and said another. That was the beginning of the end of our relationship.

A few weeks after this, I left the country to work for a non-profit in Peru for the summer. Not long after I arrived, Jordan told me via email that our relationship wasn't going to work for him. Since I couldn't be in a real relationship with him, things between us needed to change. I understood, but I was devastated. Jordan immediately began to withdraw, and this person that had been so constant in my life over the last five months and had made me so happy was now conspicuously absent. It really hurt. I was mad at him and I was mad at the Church. I felt like it was the Church that was keeping us apart. I still read the scriptures every day and prayed and attended my meetings, but I just wished none of it was true because it was causing me so much pain. I have lived away from my family for most of my adult life and I have never been homesick, but at that moment I needed my family so badly. I missed them terribly. I needed my parents. I was supposed to be abroad for the entire summer, but I was an emotional mess and only made it to the end of June.

I flew to Arizona and then got in my car and drove to Utah. I had planned on staying with Jordan for a week. Our first evening together was awkward, and things felt so different. The next day I told him that I was willing to choose him over the Church. At that moment, I just didn't know how to live without him, and I wanted to do whatever was necessary to keep him in my life. Jordan, being incredibly wise, said, "Ben, I know you better than that. You'd choose the Church over me again in the future." He was right, but hearing that broke me. Not only was losing Jordan painful, but the reality of my future, absent of true, deep human connection, felt like a weight I could not carry.

Feeling the most lost I've ever felt, I got in my car and drove to the temple. I said an audible prayer on the drive begging God to grant me some kind of deliverance. I was trying so hard to be good and yet my life was crumbling around me. Before the session started, I flipped through the Doctrine and Covenants searching for answers and came across D&C 132:50. "Behold, I have seen your sacrifices, and will forgive all your sins; I have seen your sacrifices in obedience to that which I have told you. Go, therefore, and I make a way for your escape, as I accepted the offering of Abraham of his son Isaac." It was as if God was speaking directly to me. He knew what I was feeling. He recognized my pain and my efforts to be faithful. Not only had He seen my sacrifices, but He was promising a way for me to escape a future that felt bleak and lonely.

I walked into the session wondering what escape God had prepared for me. As soon as the session started, I wanted to leave. I knew what *I* wanted the escape to be. I wanted God to tell me it was His will that I leave the Church, that I could escape from all the things that were keeping me from being with Jordan. As I sat and thought about what my life with Jordan would be like, I felt unsettled. Then I thought about my parents and going home to see them and felt a warmth bubble up inside. I pushed that feeling away because I didn't want going home to be right. I wanted to stay in Utah with Jordan. But the more I thought about going home, the more I felt drawn to the idea. Towards the end of the session I made a few firm commitments, and I felt the Spirit confirm that those commitments were the path I should take. I had entered the temple feeling completely lost, and I walked out knowing what my next steps would be.

I went back to Jordan's house and told him I'd be leaving the next morning. It was not the choice I wanted to make, but I knew I had to get home as soon as possible. He was kind that day, just as he had always been. He wanted me to do what I felt was right. Long before I met Jordan, I had made a commitment to move forward in the Church, and with that choice I knew that I was giving up the possibility of a relationship with a man. There was this vague concept of something that I was willing to give up for what I believed was true. But at the time it was an abstract sacrifice. There was nothing abstract about my current situation. The connection that I had been yearning for for so many years was in my grasp. Not the *idea* of a person to love and share my life with, but the real, corporeal, tangible, too-much-cologne-wearing Jordan. And giving him up was so much more gut-wrenching than giving up a concept. The next morning I got in my car and drove thirteen hours to my parents' house. I still felt broken, sad, and lost, but not completely hopeless. I had a small inkling of what my next steps would be.

Lehi taught that we need to see the choices that are offered to us before we can really understand the implications of the path we take. Sacrificing the idea of a relationship isn't the same as giving up a tangible person. What I learned from this relationship allowed me to choose to move forward in the Church in a way that I couldn't have had I not had that experience. And yet, at the point when I was most vulnerable and most afraid, I was ready to choose Jordan over the Church. He knew me well enough to know that that choice was not coming from the authentic parts of me, and he was wise enough and kind enough to let me go. I was one Jordan's-choice away from leaving the Church. The reality is that my relationship with Jordan was one of the sweetest experiences of my life. It also produced the most bitter pain I have ever felt. This part of my mortal experience carved out in me a new capacity for emotional depth that I had not been capable of before. And that knowledge came at a steep price as I walked out of my own innocent garden into the real world. Elder Neal A. Maxwell put it well when he taught, "The cavity which suffering carves into our souls will one day also be the receptacle of joy."[1] I don't know what choices are right for others, and I wouldn't pretend to know what choices other people should make, but I'm grateful I had this time with Jordan because it taught me to understand myself more deeply.

I am not worried that my telling this story will lead other gay members of the Church to pursue a relationship similar to the one I pursued with Jordan. What I have found from talking to many hundreds of gay Latter-day Saints is that they tend to do what they want to do regardless of my life and choices. And I'm grateful for that, because I want everyone to seek guidance and inspiration on their own journey. I have also seen that the majority of gay Latter-day Saints I know pursue a same-sex relationship at some point in their journey. I hope that my story can help straight members see what it was like for me to feel a deep connection and love for another person and how that experience helped me to grow. It was important to my progress in mortality. I am not alone in being on the verge of choosing a person that I loved over a church that I loved. However, being in this relationship was not the destination of my journey.

I don't know how to label what happened between me and Jordan. We never went on a date, so it feels incorrect to say that we dated. I also turned down his multiple requests to be boyfriends. But we had a deep connection and were definitely in love. Jordan and I are still good friends, which might seem odd. It took a few years for us to be able to be close again, after we had both moved on from the romantic parts of the relationship.

1 Neal A. Maxwell, "But for a Small Moment" (Brigham Young University devotional, Sept. 1, 1974), speeches.byu.edu.

Jordan distanced himself from the Church years ago, while I have remained an active part of it. It was hard on me that he left. It felt like a personal attack. He has told me that my staying was hard on him, that everything about my choice felt wrong. Our lives are very different, but these differences have never gotten in the way of having a real, respectful, delightful friendship. Walking different paths doesn't mean that we need to exclude each other from our lives. Even though we have our differences, I'd rather have him in my life than let our differences separate us.

Every relationship involves feelings and choosing how to act upon those feelings. Asking "have you ever acted on it?" removes the personal nature of the relationship. It removes the complexities of the people and circumstances involved and reduces human interaction to behavior. The impact this question had on me was to make me believe that if I did "act on it," I couldn't participate in the Church anymore. I didn't realize at the time that being in this relationship did not disqualify me from participating in the Church—in fact, it ultimately helped me to move forward in the Church.

As a gay person, I express love in the same ways that heterosexual people do. I hope that instead of tiptoeing around this reality by using the euphemism "acting on it," we can just use the words we would use when discussing any other relationship: dating, holding hands, kissing, falling in love. Not using those words doesn't prevent people from acting. It just increases the distance between action and compassion. Jordan acted on his feelings by doing the kindest thing he could have done—letting me go. I acted on my feelings by making the choices that made the most sense to me. When our relationship ended, I began to ask myself, *How does God act on His feelings for me? And how is He inviting me to use my agency?*

HONORING AGENCY

What have you learned about agency?

*Next to the bestowal of life itself, the right to
direct that life is God's greatest gift to man.*
-DAVID O. MCKAY, in Conference Report, Apr. 1950

When I was in high school, my brother Jay was dating a
woman that my sister and I did not like. For some reason we were
convinced that they were going to come home one night and an-
nounce that they were engaged. My sister asked my dad what we
should say if they came home showing off an engagement ring.
My dad, who didn't want them to get married either, said, "We
will cheer for them and be happy. They're going to do what they
want to do whether we like it or not. But we get to choose how
much they will be in our lives." If we wanted to stay close to our
brother, we needed to be happy when he was happy.

My dad's lesson stayed with me. I knew that no matter what
I chose, he would support and love me. I arrived at my parents'
home at eleven o'clock at night, thirteen hours after leaving
Jordan's house. The drive from Utah to Washington had been
miserable. I was heartbroken over Jordan. I sprawled out on the
living room floor, exhausted from the drive and emotionally worn
out. I was too tired to pretend to be happy and too sad to do

much besides complain. Even though I had had multiple spiritual experiences filling me with hope for the future and divine assurance that all would be well, it was sometimes hard to remember those moments when I needed them. I was thirty years old, and it felt like my life would be perpetually filled with loneliness. After things with Jordan ended, I felt a hole inside of me—an actual pit in my stomach that physically hurt.

I had come out to my parents seven years before, but we had talked very little about my orientation since that day. After our initial conversation, about once a year my dad would ask, "So how's that whole 'same-sex-attraction' thing going?" and I'd reply, "Good." My mom would hug me and tell me she loved me, and that was all we ever said about it. I just didn't feel like opening up to them. Now, seven years later, I was sitting on the same couch that I had sat on when I came out to them, and I just spewed seven years of experiences. My parents knew Jordan well, but they had been completely unaware that we'd had a romantic relationship. I told them everything that had happened and could see empathy in their eyes.

After listening for quite some time, my mom seemed to grasp how hard the last seven years had been for me. She promised, "Ben, we're not just on your side. We're with you one hundred percent. If you choose to marry a man, you and he will always be part of our family." My dad nodded his head in agreement. Until that moment, I didn't know how much I needed to hear that from my mom. I had felt trapped in a doctrine and culture that seemed to have no place for a gay man like me, wedged between wanting to be in a same-sex relationship and wanting to stay in the Church. Hearing my mom tell me that she would support me in my choices set me free. She honored my agency, just as my Heavenly Parents do. She also reassured me that if I made a choice that was outside of our doctrine, I wouldn't be outside of our family. My mother gave me life and then gave me the freedom to live it.

The Lord revealed to Joseph Smith, "All truth is independent in that sphere in which God has placed it, to act for itself" (D&C 93:30). My mother acted within her sphere of influence, as the matriarch of our family, to let me know that I would always be part of the family. She used her agency to honor mine. Now I had the freedom in my sphere to use my agency and choose which course my life would take.

I was on summer break from the University of Arizona, so I spent nearly a month at my parents' house trying to figure out what my next steps should be. I journaled a lot during the next few weeks. After a long conversation with my dad in which we both spilled our guts, I wrote, "What I really appreciate about my dad is that he asks really good questions and he listens. He's also thought deeply about this stuff. It felt so good to be 100% honest with him and for each of us to just share our feelings and be on the same page." In the seven years since I had come out to him, my dad had spent many hours reading stories of gay Latter-day Saints. Familiarizing himself with the stories of others helped him know how to listen to and relate to mine. He had prepared himself for a conversation that initially neither he nor I was ready to have. The next day, I wrote, "Went to the temple with my parents, which was great. However, my mom spends a little too much time looking at me lovingly."

During this time, I would wake up in the morning and not want to get out of bed. The hole inside of me weighed me down. I called a friend and told her that I understood why it's called heartbreak—it felt like something inside of me was actually broken. Even though I had dated women before, none of the breakups had felt anything like this. I asked her how long it would hurt, and she said, "For a couple of months." I whined and told her I wanted to get over it now. She wisely explained that that isn't how this works. "Losing a piece of you is painful," she said, "and it hurts for a while."

After opening up to my parents, I decided to have some frank conversations with my siblings as well. I initially came out to my sister Lindsay when I was twenty-five. This was not information that she had been expecting. "Lindsay, remember how much I loved *The Golden Girls* and *My Little Pony*?" As she thought about all the signals throughout the years that pointed to my being gay, things clicked. The following day she gave me a beautiful letter that she had written the evening after I came out to her. Part of the letter said she hoped I would always live close to her so that I could be an integral part of her family. We didn't talk about my orientation much in the next five years. Now that I was "in the depths of despair," as Anne Shirley would say, I needed to open up to her. She knew Jordan well, and I told her all about my relationship with him. Then I asked if she thought I should try to date another guy. She answered, "Do whatever you feel is right and makes you happy. If it's the right thing for you, then I'm all for it."

I wrote in my journal that night, "I have a marvelous sister." Her expression of trust in me not only felt good and affirming, but it gave me the freedom to explore what the right thing was for me. I also wrote in my journal that I couldn't envision a future in which I wasn't part of the Church.

I had a similar conversation with my brother Jessen and my sister-in-law Laura. Jessen said that he would support me if I decided to leave the Church, but he also said that he didn't think that decision would make me happy. He did not say it in a preachy way, but in a way that showed his sincere concern for me. I didn't need my family to be excited if I left the Church. I didn't need them to fully embrace the idea of me being in a same-sex marriage. I needed them to try to understand my life and be with me as I wrestled with these tough choices. I loved that they let me be me and didn't expect me to have it all figured out. As Elder Dieter F. Uchtdorf taught, "In this Church that honors personal agency so strongly, . . . we respect those who honestly search for truth. It may break our hearts when their journey takes them away from the Church we love and the truth we have found, but we honor their right to worship Almighty God according to the dictates of their own conscience, just as we claim that privilege for ourselves" ("Come, Join with Us," *Ensign*, Nov. 2013). I appreciated Jessen's honest assessment that I would be happier moving forward in the Church. What else could I expect him to say? His authentic assessment of my circumstances was what I wanted. His honesty coupled with his effort to understand were exactly what I needed.

Out of everyone in my family, Jessen and Laura were the closest with Jordan, and they were really interested in what our relationship had been like. I was pretty honest with them, even revealing that we had kissed and held hands. Laura thought it was cute and could see how we would have such a great connection. Jessen's response was to involuntarily shudder and say, "Sorry to make light of this, but yuck! I mean, if that works for you, great, but I just don't get it."

I think it's fair to say that my brother's reaction could be considered unkind. However, he was simply being honest, and I'm so glad he was honest with me. As I was pleading for the freedom to be open and honest, I'm grateful that Jessen was, too. His undisguised reaction was more meaningful to me than a dishonest reaction, or him just saying something to please me. I like what President Hugh B. Brown said: "We are not so much concerned with whether your thoughts are orthodox or heterodox as we are that you shall have thoughts."[1]

I wasn't so concerned with whether or not my family members reacted by shuddering or rejoicing as I talked about my love life. Instead I cared that they were willing to have the conversation at all. However, I would hope that those close to me would not react with revulsion when I open up to them about my life. I know my brother's reaction would be different now, years later. He works as a school counselor and started a club at his school for LGBTQ students. As he was telling me about this club, he said, "I did it for you, Ben. I don't want anyone to feel as lonely as you felt, and I want to be there for the kids that need support."

My brother Jay was the last person in the family I came out to. He and I don't typically sit down and have deep conversations, but we get along great and are super similar. I often joke that he's living my straight life. I had trouble opening up to him because I felt like he was more concerned about me staying in the Church and the strength of my testimony than he was about really understanding me. Because of this, I didn't really tell him a lot of what was going on. I didn't feel like he understood what it was like for me to be a gay member of the Church. I didn't have a heart-to-heart with Jay that summer like I did with everyone else in my family because neither of us opened the door to have that kind of conversation. In the years since, he and I have spoken at length. After Jay was called to serve in a stake presidency, he would occasionally email me questions about LGBTQ topics. I remember him calling me on the phone to tell me a bunch of epiphanies he'd had after

---

1 Hugh B. Brown, "An Eternal Quest—Freedom of the Mind" (Brigham Young University devotional, May 13, 1969), speeches.byu.edu.

sharing some of my insights in a stake training he'd given. He said he was beginning to understand the sacrifice I was making by staying in the Church. Jay told me that when he thought of what it meant to endure to the end, he would think of me.

That summer at my parents' house, I searched the scriptures for answers. I sat in the rec room with my scriptures opened on my lap. As I read, the hole inside of me started to fill in. Then I would stop and the pain would return. This pattern led me to spend a lot of time in the word of God trying to heal my broken heart. I read the words of Jesus in Gethsemane: "Father, if thou be willing, remove this cup from me: nevertheless not my will, but thine, be done" (Luke 22:42). I thought to myself, *I don't want to have to choose between being in the Church and being with someone I love.* The cup I had been given felt so incredibly unfair. And yet the Savior acted in His sphere of influence to drink from a cup that He didn't want. What cup was God offering me?

I opened up the Book of Mormon and read: "Therefore, cheer up your hearts, and remember that ye are free to act for yourselves" (2 Nephi 10:23). God had given me a set of choices, and I was the only one who could decide what to do. Nephi taught that I should be glad that no one could choose for me. The next verse led me to earnestly seek God's will: "Wherefore, my beloved brethren, reconcile yourselves to the will of God, and not to the will of the devil and the flesh; and remember, after ye are reconciled unto God, that it is only in and through the grace of God that ye are saved" (v. 24). I had been focusing so much on my pain, my loneliness, and my desperation that I had failed to really ascertain the will of God regarding my orientation. I had been so intent on *changing* who I was that I missed out on *being* who I was.

As I sought God's will and turned to Christ, I felt Christ

point me to His Church and the promises I had made. I felt called to keep my covenants to obey God, to live His gospel, to keep the law of chastity, and to consecrate my life to building His kingdom. I felt compelled to act within my sphere of influence to choose to live the restored gospel. For the first time in my life, I felt settled that changing my sexual orientation was outside of my sphere of influence. God wasn't asking me to change that part of me. He was inviting me to be the person He created me to be. And so, even though it was a bitter decision at the time, I chose to drink in a renewed commitment to a life within the teachings of The Church of Jesus Christ of Latter-day Saints.

After a month of staying with my family, the time came to head back to Arizona and return to real life. As I drove by myself to Arizona, I concluded that I couldn't keep doing things the way I had before. It hadn't worked. My mind and my spirit were both telling me, through the pain I was in, that something wasn't right. Similar to how our bodies give us hunger pangs to tell us to nourish ourselves, my spirit was telling me that something needed to change. While keeping my sexual orientation a secret had been hard on me, the real cancer was the shame it created. What would people think of me if they knew I was gay? Would they hate me like I had hated myself? I couldn't let fear control me anymore. I couldn't live with the shame anymore. So over the next six months, I came out to every person I was close to in my life. I made a lot of phone calls, had a lot of one-on-one conversations, and wrote a lot of emails. And I sent a few letters.

One of the letters I sent was to the Wrights in Orem, Utah. Martin and Cyndi are Craig's aunt and uncle. When Craig and I were roommates, they'd had us over once a month for Sunday dinner. Then Craig got married and moved away, but they kept inviting me. Then I moved away, but every time I passed through

Utah I stayed at their house. With my parents and siblings far away in Washington, the Wright family had taken me in long before they knew I was gay. They made sure I always had a place to spend holidays and eat Sunday dinners. I sent the letter, wondering how this disclosure was about to change our relationship. A week later I got a letter back from Cyndi. It said in part: "Thank you so much for your letter. We really appreciate you sharing your story with us. Nothing changes. We still love you as one of our own." Cyndi used her agency to choose me. She acted within her sphere of influence to let me know that I was family. While some families put distance between themselves and their gay loved ones, the Wrights chose to keep me close.

The next time I was in Utah, I stayed at the Wrights' house. Cyndi and I stayed up talking after everyone else had gone to bed. She reiterated what she had said in the letter: that I was family. She told me that no matter which path I chose, she would always claim me. I had wasted a lot of time worrying what other people would think of me. I wondered why I was having so many positive experiences coming out when I had heard so many negative stories.

These choices I was making were deeply personal and mine to make. I'm not advocating that anyone should simply mirror the way I exercise my agency. The God-given gift of agency requires all free agents to do their own spiritual work to reconcile themselves with the will of God, whatever that is for them and their lives. As the Lord spoke to me through His authorized servants, through the scriptures, and through the Holy Ghost, I was led down the path that was right for me. The key for me was to be connected enough to heaven that I could be guided on how to proceed in my unique circumstances.

To paraphrase David O. McKay, the most precious gift we

have been given, next to life itself, is the power to direct that life. "All truth is independent in that sphere in which God has placed it, to act for itself, as all intelligence also; *otherwise there is no existence*" (D&C 93:30; emphasis added). Our Heavenly Parents endowed us with life and with the gift of agency. If we don't have agency, we don't exist. That is, if we cannot act independently of God's will for us, then we can't really act upon His will, or our own free will, either. It must be terrifying even for Heavenly Parents to let Their children act for themselves. And yet They enabled us to do so. They gave us existence. They didn't just create us materially. They gave us power to act for ourselves. I think of Them observing me during those weeks I spent with my earthly parents, weeping with me and pleading with me to use my agency wisely. I imagine them cheering for my family members when, like Them, they promised to always honor my agency. I think of Them watching Cyndi pen that letter promising to always claim me and imagine Them saying, "We will always claim you too, Ben."

While I have not chosen my sexual orientation, I do have a multitude of other choices. As a gay Latter-day Saint, the choice I make again and again is to seek out God's will for me and then to do it. I believe that the Lord wants us to honor one another's agency as He does. We can't exist without agency. Our relationships can't thrive without the freedom to choose. I was blessed by my loved ones when they explicitly told me that they wanted me in their families no matter what I chose. Hearing them say those things changed my life. Those affirmations took me from a pit of despair and offered me hope. I doubt my mom or Cyndi or the many other people in my life who said similar things recognized the gift they were offering me in those moments. But I know it now. And our Heavenly Parents knew it all along.

A CLOUD OF WITNESSES

What is the value of bringing LGBTQ people together?

*Unless someone like you cares a whole
awful lot, nothing is going to get better. It's not.*

–DR. SEUSS, *The Lorax* (New York: Random House), 1971

While cleaning my house in Tucson one morning, I listened to a presentation by Tom Christofferson. Tom shared his journey of coming to terms with his sexuality and leaving the Church for thirty years. He also shared the story of his friend John Gustav-Wrathall. Both had been excommunicated in their twenties. Both had felt the Spirit pull them back to Church activity after being away for years. Both were committed to truth and doing the will of God. And then their paths diverged. Tom ended his relationship with his partner, and John stayed with his husband. Tom made the decision to be rebaptized. John wanted to be rebaptized, yet felt that he should keep his family intact while continuing to attend church. Two people earnestly seeking God's will received two different answers on what to do. I wondered, how could this be?

As I listened to Tom share his story and John's story, I felt a clear impression from the Spirit. I would articulate the feeling this way: "Ben, you believe in the Restoration just as much as

Tom and John do. If you left the Church, you would eventually come back, too. Just skip the excommunication part and stay the whole time." I knew at my core that this was true, that I would always return. I had once again been wondering what my future in the Church could look like, wondering how to find joy in a single life. It suddenly became clear yet again that the right course for me was to move forward in the Church. Their examples helped me to plot out my own course, and their witnesses of the Restoration confirmed mine.

The Apostle Paul shares multiple stories in Hebrews 11 of ancient Saints who had faith in God. Then he says, "Wherefore seeing we also are compassed about with so great a cloud of witnesses, let us lay aside every weight, and the sin which doth so easily beset us, and let us run with patience the race that is set before us" (Hebrews 12:1). Paul explains that being surrounded by the witness of others can lighten us, give us courage to abandon sin, and help us to pursue the course that is laid out for us. Surrounding myself that morning in the testimonies of Tom and John had helped me see the race that I was called to run. Hearing their experiences allowed me to receive personal revelation about my own life. They had answered a call to share their experiences, and I was better because they had shared their stories. I felt a similar call while walking in the rain a few days after Christmas.

I started my blog in 2008 at the insistence of my friend Joleen. I'd just come back from spending the summer doing an internship in Mexico and was telling her and another friend about all the entertaining things that had happened while I was there. Joleen told me I should start a blog about the funny things that happened to me so she wouldn't miss out on anything. Being an obliging friend, that's exactly what I did. For the next six years I blogged about anything I thought would be entertaining. I blogged about my adventures substitute teaching. I blogged about borrowing a goat to eat the weeds in my backyard. I blogged about my house that looked straight out of the '70s. I blogged about my summer in Portugal. I blogged about hanging out with my sister. Really riveting stuff. Occasionally, I would write serious things, but it was primarily a humor space. Then I was home in Washington visiting my parents in 2014 for Christmas. I went on a walk in the rain one evening to get out of the house and listen to a podcast. The host gave an impassioned plea for everyone to tell their stories. He said that telling stories would change the world. I felt a jolt to my system. I needed to share my story, and I needed to share it on my blog.

A year earlier, I had written an essay about coming out to Mitch and Craig in Kiwanis Park for a *BYU Studies* alumni essay contest. I submitted it to the contest, and it promptly lost. I had felt inspired to write it believing that it would get published and do some good. I didn't understand why God had asked me to write something that no one would read. At the time, most of the people in my life didn't know I was gay. I began to share this essay with friends and loved ones whenever I came out to them. It was a helpful tool that allowed them to walk in my shoes a bit without me having to tell the same story again and again. As I walked in the rain, I knew that I had to share this essay on my blog. I told my parents that I was going to post the essay, and I talked to everyone mentioned in the essay to get their permission. Besides a handful of other people that were important to me, no one else knew that I was going to come out publicly.

I sat in my parents' rec room a week later with the post ready to publish, wondering if this was really what I was supposed to do. I was terrified. My dream for years had been to work at the MTC as an administrator. I was in the middle of getting a PhD in Second Language Acquisition and Teaching to prepare for this. There was no way, I thought, that the MTC would hire an openly gay man. I felt that by publishing this post I would be giving up my dream career. As the only Ben Schilaty on the internet, I'm super Google-able. Once I put this information out there, I couldn't take it back. So I said a fervent prayer asking God if I was really supposed to do this. There is a very specific feeling I get when I know I'm supposed to bear my testimony. It's like a nervous, courageous sort of feeling. As I prayed, I got that feeling times ten. I knew I had to do it. So I pushed publish, I shared the link on my Facebook page, and I closed my laptop. I walked into the kitchen and said to my parents, "I gotta get out of here. I don't want to think about what I just did." So I turned off my phone and we went to see a movie so I could escape reality for a few hours.

When we got home, I turned on my phone. It had been on for less than twenty seconds when I got a call from a high school friend who doesn't even have Facebook. Her sister, who I hadn't talked to in years, had seen the post and told her to call me. This friend isn't a Latter-day Saint. She told me how proud of me she was for finally being open. She had assumed for years that I was gay, and now, twelve years after high school, she was glad I was finally coming out. As she and I talked on the phone and caught up, my phone dinged again and again and again. When I got off the phone, I sifted through dozens of text messages, emails, voicemails, and Facebook messages from friends who had read the post sending me their love and support. I went to the Facebook post and read all the comments and went through the list of who had "liked" the post. Something happened that I hadn't anticipated. As I went through all the names, I thought, *She knows, I don't have to lie to her anymore. He knows, I can be myself around him now.* It was an incredibly freeing experience knowing that I didn't have to hide anymore. An enormous weight came off my shoulders, and I felt a newfound freedom as I began to share my story.

Over the next few days, my post started getting shared around, and I began to get emails from strangers. I received about two dozen of them. They all said roughly the same thing: "I'm a gay member of the Church. No one knows. I read your post and thought I should reach out to you." These people were from all over the country. I responded to every email saying that they could reach out whenever they wanted. I realized, however, that there wasn't a ton I could do to help people in faraway places. Then I realized that I was the only gay Latter-day Saint I knew of in Tucson, but in a city with multiple stakes, there was no way that I was the only one.

When I returned from Christmas break, I sent an email to my stake president, Lee Walker. I explained that I wanted to start a group similar to the Genesis Group, which was started in the early '70s for Black members of the Church. They held a monthly meeting where Black Latter-day Saints and their friends could build their faith in Christ together and be with people who'd had similar life experiences. I told President Walker that I wanted to start a group like this for the LGBTQ members of our stake. He and I didn't really know each other, but he set up a meeting to talk with me. When we met, we talked about my vision and what I wanted the group to look like. He had a lot of questions but was supportive of the idea. And then he did something I hadn't expected—he called me to a stake calling. I was still pretty new to being out publicly at this point. I had published my blog post only a few weeks before, so I was still working through a lot of insecurities. I couldn't believe that President Walker knew I was gay and still trusted me to serve in a stake-wide assignment. I cried that night as I wrote about it in my journal. I was still learning that people could know about my orientation and yet fully trust and respect me. I was thirty-one years old.

The stake wasn't able to officially sponsor the group, but we had President Walker's full support to move forward independently, and he asked a high councilor to work with us. Our first meeting was small, but we grew pretty quickly. As word spread about the group, people started to show up. The original plan was to have a gospel-centered meeting once a month and a social once a month. It turned out that we all became good friends and hung out all the time, so there was no need to hold formal socials. But once a month we'd get together to discuss the gospel.

When new people would come to the group, I'd usually take them on a walk or to dinner so that I could get to know them better. Tucson has dry riverbeds called washes that only have water in them when it rains. There are walkways along the larger ones, and I walked many, many miles along these rivers in Tucson listening to my friends and hearing their stories. One of these new friends was Jeremy. As he and I walked and chatted, he repeatedly apologized for talking about himself so much. I said, "It's okay. Get it all out. No need to apologize." This was the first time he'd been able to talk to someone who understood a bit of what it was like to be him.

Jeremy later told me in an email how my story had helped him. He wrote in part: "I was shocked to read your story and finally see that there was someone that had somewhat similar experiences and wanted to live the gospel. I had prayed for three years to be able to talk to someone that could understand exactly how I felt, tell them how I felt, and support what I wanted to do. I really didn't think someone like that existed." He wrote me a letter years later, for my thirty-sixth birthday. He said: "You gave me the gift to truly be and accept myself. I'm not perfect at it yet, but I am so much better than before. I don't feel as though I could ever express how grateful I am for that. That first walk along the river will always be one of my favorite memories." Years later, these moments of openness and friendship still mean so much to both of us. We needed to be in each other's lives.

Another member of the group invited me to her apartment for lunch. She told me all about her life out of the Church and why she had recently chosen to return. She apologized multiple times for sharing unsavory details, and I encouraged her to tell her story the way she wanted to. It was her first experience really talking about being a queer Latter-day Saint. She had a lot of great questions, and we talked about the importance of following the Spirit and how God gives us many chances to do the right thing. She told me how grateful she was for me and how good it felt to talk. As I walked to my car after lunch, I felt a huge wave of gratitude that I had been privileged to be in this person's life and be part of her journey. I got a little emotional as I considered the sacred experience of being present for her witness.

I initially thought that everyone would lean on me as the oldest member and founder of the group. But they didn't need me—we needed each other. I marveled as I saw members of the group support each other. People with varied interests and seemingly incompatible personalities became dear friends. The tone of my journal shifted in the months after starting the group. It became filled with entries about how amazing and full my life was. For example, on December 12, 2016, I wrote, "I just spent tonight hanging out with friends. I have a wonderful life." Looking back on my earlier journals, the ones filled with pages of fear and self-loathing, I can barely recognize myself. These entries from my time in Tucson sound so much more like me—entries where I'm happy and thriving and living my best life. The pages of my journal are filled with gratitude for the people in my life. We became more than friends. We became family.

My last semester at the University of Arizona I decided I wanted to read the whole Book of Mormon. I invited everyone in the group to join me. I did the math and figured that we had to read five pages a day to finish before graduation. Jeremy made a reading chart and bought a bunch of stickers so we could keep track of our reading. We got together multiple times a week to discuss what we were reading and how it related to us as LGBTQ Church members. During one discussion I joked, "Do you think Ammon was gay? The king offered for him to marry his daughter and he replied: 'Marry the princess?! Can I just be your servant instead?'" For me, sharing my faith with others who shared my sexual orientation was a powerful, beautiful experience. And it was a lot of fun, too.

One morning a new member of the group texted me after attending Book of Mormon study the night before. Something that someone had said at the meeting really got him thinking. He came over that night to talk, and so did Jeremy. He unloaded a lot of his struggles onto us, and my heart wept for him. He told us that he felt conflicted and broken. He cried as he confided that he hated being gay and was mad at God for making him gay. He told Jeremy and me that he was shocked to find a group of gay Latter-day Saints because he didn't think that was possible. Then he asked us for a blessing. The Spirit in the room was palpable as two gay priesthood holders laid our hands on the head of another gay Latter-day Saint to give him a blessing. I pondered on how a loving God endowed His children with power so that I, a fellow gay man, was able to be a voice for Heavenly Father to assure my friend he was loved just as he was. I don't think that message would have been as powerful coming from a straight person.

Group members would sometimes share stories of hurtful things that were said at church or by Church members about LGBTQ people. Paul, one of the original members of the group, told me more than once that we needed to do something to help straight members of the Church understand the LGBTQ Latter-day Saint experience. In December 2015 he asked if he could invite some straight friends over to my house to share his story. I initially didn't see how this would help, but eight people showed up on a Sunday night. We sat in a circle as Paul spent twenty minutes sharing his gay Latter-day Saint story and then let people ask him questions. It was an awesome, uplifting, soul-expanding experience. He asked if we could do it again the next week, and I was thrilled. He invited a different group of people, he shared his story for twenty minutes, and then he again let his friends ask him questions. Both nights the Spirit was strong as Paul opened up his heart and his friends sincerely tried to understand. These nights felt like Zion as the people in the room became more "of one heart and one mind" (Moses 7:18).

Paul invited me to share my story the next time. We each took ten minutes to share and then let people ask us questions. Again it was a beautiful experience. As more and more LGBTQ members began to feel comfortable, they started sharing their stories, too. The cloud of witnesses grew. We began to call these meetings in people's homes Ally Nights because we were helping straight members of the Church understand how they could be good allies to their LGBTQ friends and loved ones. After one Ally Night, Ryleigh pointed out something that I hadn't noticed. Only gay men were telling their stories. Ryleigh is a private person and doesn't like attention, but she felt she needed to start sharing her story, too. Not only did she point out a blind spot that I hadn't noticed, but she provided a perspective that hadn't yet been shared. She courageously shared her experiences, and as she opened her heart, our hearts were knit with hers.

We hosted dozens and dozens of Ally Nights all over Tucson. My entire stake presidency took ninety minutes of their time to sit in my living room and hear two gay members of the stake share their stories. They asked some really beautiful questions. My bishop came to one as well. One of the young single adult wards had a number of active LGBTQ members. Each member of the bishopric of that ward hosted an Ally Night in his home. The women and men from my stake who supported and hosted these events are my heroes, because they elevated our voices. Hundreds of people came to listen, understand, and see what they could do better. We started a conversation that hadn't been happening before. On multiple occasions, people told me that after attending Ally Night, someone they knew had come out to them, and because they had come to the meeting, they knew how to respond. Often people stayed long after the meeting to ask further questions and just to get to know one another better. Hundreds of Saints got together to hear their sisters and brothers share what was in their hearts.

Each Ally Night ended with everyone in the room sharing a takeaway from the night. Often these takeaways weren't about what was said, but a message that was received through the Holy Ghost. During the takeaways one evening, a friend of mine mentioned that everyone just wants to be understood. She told the group that she suffered from depression and that it's hard when people tell her to just choose to be happy. A few weeks later I ran into her at the institute. She told me that she had just been in Utah visiting some friends. Some of her friends had said that people choose to be gay. She took a deep breath and said to herself, *Okay, time to be an ally.* Then she shared the insight she had had at Ally Night. Just like it wouldn't be right to tell a person with depression to just choose to be happy, it wouldn't be right to tell a gay person to just choose to be straight. My heart swelled with gratitude for this friend of mine who had not only taken the time to learn about our experiences but had stood up for truth and corrected misinformation. She's my hero, too.

At an Ally Night at a bishop's house, Jeremy shared his story for the first time and I spoke as well. As we went around the room sharing our takeaways from the night, a woman whom I hadn't met before said, "I want to thank you two for being so open and honest tonight. I want you to know that I am going to be an LGBTQ ally and I will support you no matter which path you choose. I know many of you don't have families in town, and I will be your Tucson mom if you need one. Call me any time, day or night, and I will be there for you. The doors to my home are always open to you, and you are part of my family now." After the meeting she gave us both big hugs and thanked us for being so brave and reiterated that she would be there for us. As the cloud of witnesses in Tucson grew, so did the expressions of love and support. I wish every gay Latter-day Saint could hear the messages that I consistently heard from straight Latter-day Saints in Tucson. "We love you. We claim you. You are one of us. You belong in this Church." We didn't start Ally Night expecting these kinds of compassionate responses, but they are simply the natural reaction to understanding our stories.

Jeremy's mom attended an Ally Night and asked how same-sex attraction fits into the plan of salvation. This led to a long, deep discussion. Another mom was there with her teenage son, who had recently come out to the family. During the takeaways she said that she'd never really thought about same-sex attraction and the plan of salvation before. Then she said that she just wants her son to be happy and will be with him on whichever path he chooses. The son then said, "Oh, Mom, you're gonna make me cry." Then he thanked everyone for giving him hope. And he did cry. Jeremy told me later that the meeting had really helped his mom understand things better. Openly sharing our stories helped two moms to better understand and connect with their sons. Ally Nights were a spiritual thrill every time.

My friends who courageously shared their witnesses are pioneers to me. As the Primary song "To Be a Pioneer" (*Children's Songbook*, 218) teaches:

> *You don't have to push a handcart,*
> *Leave your fam'ly dear,*
> *Or walk a thousand miles or more*
> *To be a pioneer!*
> *You do need to have great courage,*
> *Faith to conquer fear,*
> *And work with might for a cause that's right*
> *To be a pioneer!*

I ran the LGBTQ support group for two years until I moved away from Tucson. For the last meeting I invited everyone to read "The Living Christ," which we then discussed as a group. I asked the group: If there were a paragraph added to the document about LGBTQ people, what would it say? The unanimous answer was that it would say that the living Christ loves us. We then talked about how we had all learned that we are loved by God. Then, out of nowhere, Jeremy pulled out a poem he had written and read it to the group. He spoke of feeling so broken and alone, and how our time together had put the broken pieces of him back together and given him hope. He talked about how our speaking up and walking together had opened up a new world to him that was full of possibilities. It was a real gift that he shared with us that night.

In my final lesson to the group, I told everyone that I hadn't planned to start an organization that would be self-perpetuating. That wasn't what I was asked to do. But Heavenly Father had told me that there were people in Tucson at that time that needed each other. Within a year of my moving away, almost everyone else moved away as well. Whenever I run into someone from the Tucson LGBTQ group, it's like reuniting with family. Those two years were a golden age for me. Easily some of the happiest, most rewarding times in my life.

My last semester in Tucson, I was speaking to Brother Bauer, the institute director, after an Ally Night that he had attended. A student had recently told him how cool it was that there were so many openly gay students at the institute. Brother Bauer thanked me and said that my friends and I had made that possible—that we had started a conversation in Tucson that hadn't been happening before. Later that night I was talking to Paul, who had the idea to start Ally Nights. I said, "You did that, Paul. We did this." Then I thought for a moment and said, "No, God did this through us."

THE POLICY

What do you do when church hurts?

The First Presidency and Quorum of the Twelve have continued to seek the Lord's guidance and to plead with Him in behalf of His children who were affected by the 2015 policy. We knew that this policy created concern and confusion for some and heartache for others. That grieved us. Whenever the sons and daughters of God weep—for whatever reasons—we weep. So our supplications to the Lord continued.

–RUSSELL M. NELSON, "The Love and Laws of God"
(Brigham Young University devotional, Sept. 17, 2019)

On Thursday, November 5, 2015, I drove from Arizona to California to visit my friends Ian and Amy. It had been more than a year since I'd seen them, so while we sat in their kitchen eating dinner and catching up on our lives I ignored the phone buzzing in my pocket. When I finally checked my phone, I had a few messages from friends in Tucson saying that the Latter-day Saint internet circles were exploding with news of a new policy from the Church. I wasn't sure what they were talking about. After some more chatting with Ian and Amy and playing with their kids for a bit, I got online to see what was going on. I was stunned to read that a new policy from the Church stated that entering into a same-sex marriage was now considered apostasy and that children of same-sex couples could not be baptized until they turned eighteen. Most of the reactions I saw online were either anger and betrayal or simply disbelief or confusion. Since the news had been leaked and hadn't come directly from the Church, a lot of people thought it was a hoax or misinformation. I decided to wait for official word from the Church to see if it was real or not.

Even though I'd known Ian and Amy for years, I had only come out to them a year earlier via email. We hadn't seen each other since then, so we spent some time talking about my experiences as a gay member of the Church and what that had meant for me. We also discussed the leaked policy at length. Soon an interview with Elder Christofferson clarifying the policy was posted, and I watched it alone in the guest room. I wanted to know what was really going on. I was hoping that he would repudiate the policy, apologize for the misinformation, and talk about how awesome his gay brother, Tom, is. But instead he justified and explained the policy. I felt sick. I had a strong testimony of Elder Christofferson's call as a special witness of the Savior, but his words still stung. I knew how much this news was going to hurt and affect people that I loved.

Memories of my time with Jordan flooded into my mind after I listened to Elder Christofferson's interview. It had been such a meaningful relationship to me. And I was willing to give it all away to do what I felt to be God's will. There was a part of me that had hoped that somehow, someday, I'd be able to live these two parts of me. On this day, however, it became even clearer that I wasn't allowed to hope for this thing that I wanted so badly. And knowing that I wasn't allowed to hope for a relationship with a man made me wish I could disappear.

I had just started the LGBTQ support group in Tucson two months before, and now I felt like there was no point in trying to help people stay in the Church. My initial thought after watching the interview was, *I don't want to do this anymore. Why am I trying to help LGBTQ members stay in the Church when Church leaders don't want us?* Elder Christofferson had said that the policy was created out of love, but all I felt was rejection. The policy wasn't about me. It didn't directly affect a single, childless person like me. But as a member of the LGBTQ community, I still felt rejected. It felt like I had been punched in the gut.

A lot of people who were upset by the policy focused on how it prohibited the children of same-sex couples from getting baptized. This wasn't the painful part for me. The painful part was the word *apostasy* and how members in same-sex marriages would be considered apostates. This experience brought up buried feelings of what I wished my life could look like. I was not in a same-sex marriage, nor did I have any plans to be, but deep down I wanted the kind of relationship that was now labeled apostasy. I really, really wanted to be in a committed relationship with a man that I loved. In fact, it was the second most earnest desire of my life. There was only one thing that trumped it—more than anything, I wanted to ascertain God's will for me and then follow it. And I had felt multiple times that He wanted me in His Church. If I wanted to stay in the Church, I couldn't have a committed relationship with a man. With this policy announcement, my desire was not only considered a sin, but it would be a sin so bad that I'd be called an apostate. This was perplexing to me because I know what it's like to feel sorrow when I sin, to want to repent, and the joy that comes when I feel I've become a better person. I thought about my time with Jordan and how we had fallen in love. Not just a crush—we really, really loved each other. And loving him didn't feel like a sin to me.

In Matthew 21, Jesus taught a parable about two sons. When their father asked the first son to go work in his vineyard, the son said he wouldn't go, but he later repented and went. The second son said he would go, but never went. Jesus then asked which of the two did the will of his father (see v. 31). Even though the first son wasn't quick to obey right from the start, the softening of his heart and his eventual repentance qualified him as doing the will of his father. I deeply identify with the first son. Sometimes I complain, express frustration, and feel like I can't do what I'm being asked to do. I am grateful that my Father offers me grace and time to grow while I align my will with His. In my heart I am often enticed to turn down divine invitations. Yet despite what I initially feel or say, I try my best to eventually respond to the call to do God's will.

I already understood that if I wanted to move forward in the Church, a same-sex marriage was off the table for me. I thought that I had accepted that fact. It was something that I didn't really think about too much. I just moved forward day to day living my life, only occasionally considering what I was giving up. Then, when the policy used the word *apostasy* to describe what I wanted, it was like the pain of what I was sacrificing was being placed right in front of me, and I was forced to look at and accept that pain. I didn't want to leave the Church, but I didn't want to have to take all this pain with me either. I went to bed that night feeling rejected and hopeless.

I woke up the next morning to a text message from a friend in Utah expressing her love for me and telling me how much she wished that we lived close to each other so she could see me regularly. She wrote in part, "What a great blessing that would be to me to have such a good friend in my life. You're the best." Over the next twenty-four hours I got Facebook messages, emails, texts, and phone calls from dozens of people asking how I was doing, expressing love for me, and telling me how much I meant to them. All these messages reminded me of the joy in my life and signaled to me that the Latter-day Saints who knew me wanted me in their Church. In my journal I recorded many of the names of the people who reached out to me, including a "random girl who read one of my old blog posts and emailed me." Those simple acts of kindness deserved to be remembered and preserved. My initial, visceral response began to go away as I saw and felt all the love and empathy that existed in my community. People wanted me in their lives.

Kevin's dad, Ken, emailed me to see how I was doing. He talked about being patient and waiting on the Lord's time. He also shared some lovely scriptures and quotes, which I really appreciated. I liked all of that, but the part that made the difference was how he ended the email: "Ben, you are part of our family and we have been so blessed to have you come into our lives. We love you so much and cherish our relationship with you here in mortality and want it to continue into the eternities." I cried, of course.

That weekend I spent a lot of time with Ian, Amy, and their kids. Their three-year-old constantly tried to get my attention by asking me silly questions like if I'd like to eat a whale. Then he'd yell, "Look at my sock!" and I'd look. Then he'd yell, "Look at my other sock!" and I'd look again. It was adorable. Amy told me how much she hoped I'd get a job in California so I could live close to them. Ian said, "I know you haven't left yet, but when are you going to come back?" Amy then suggested that I visit twice a year, and Ian amended it to at least once a quarter. It was hard to be annoyed or hurt or angry at a policy when so many wonderful people were telling me how much they wanted me in their lives. I wrote in my journal that day: "I'm hopeful and optimistic. We'll get this worked out."

I made a lot of phone calls as I drove home to Arizona. I talked to my parents, who had found the policy to be very upsetting. We had an odd role reversal in that conversation. I, their gay son, comforted them and told them that everything would be okay. I called another friend who said that the policy made him feel nasty. I called Jordan, whom I still talked to sporadically. In the year since our relationship had ended, he had continued to attend church regularly. As we talked about the policy, he said, "I cannot tolerate this." He stopped attending church. I wanted to comfort him and tell him to stay, but what could I say?

I felt tossed to and fro as I read widely divergent views of the policy online. Some said that the Church was a toxic environment and was requiring too much of its LGBTQ members. Others said that the gospel is so simple and that living it would bring joy. Some said, "If you are gay and staying in the Church, you're deluded." Others said, "Just follow the prophet, he knows the way." While all this was happening, I was engaged in a personal wrestle. Deep down I wanted to move forward in the Church *and* be in a same-sex marriage. I wanted two things, and I couldn't have them both. I wanted so desperately for the Church to say, "We want you. We claim you. You belong here." But instead it felt like the message was, "If you choose to marry a man, you're out." So I prayed and I fasted and I read and I pondered and I served and I tried to figure out what God wanted me to do. And I felt called to live my life in a way that reflected Church teachings.

There were some tough moments that fall. It wasn't constant, but the feeling that Church leaders didn't want people like me in the Church returned regularly. Some Church meetings were just plain painful. One Sunday I just couldn't sit in sacrament meeting. The talks hurt and made me angry. I was agitated, and as soon as the meeting was over I was ready to leave. I am not good at hiding my emotions. I was sitting next to Kevin's sister, and she could tell that I was not okay. I told her I just couldn't be at church and was going home. She was the Primary president at the time and said, "Just come to Primary with me, Ben." I went, and for two hours I sat on a chair that was too small for me and sang Primary songs in Spanish. As I sat there singing, the Spirit was able to start mending the broken pieces of my heart. A heart that had been broken by feeling like my Church didn't want me. When church was over, I left without talking to anyone. I just couldn't put on a happy face that day. But the Spirit had spoken to me, I had stayed, and I would come back.

The policy made national news, and my friends who weren't members of the Church had a lot of questions. I didn't know what to say. I didn't know how to defend a policy that didn't feel right in my mind or in my heart. I immediately started praying that God would change the policy. He had to. Then in January 2016, President Nelson gave a talk at BYU–Hawaii and said that the policy had come by revelation. This really shook me. It was like the scab had just been ripped off of a wound that was still healing. This thing that did not feel right to me was now being called a revelation. So I did more praying and more pondering and more studying. I decided that maybe I shouldn't pray that the policy would change, because I didn't want to "ask for that which [I] ought not" (D&C 8:10). I recognized a need for personal humility, understanding that what seemed best to me right then might not be the best. My prayers shifted from asking for God to change the policy to asking Him to send us further light and knowledge as a people. This helped me to focus less on one particular outcome and more on allowing God to teach me and His people. I was sure that God had so much more to teach us about His LGBTQ children, and I was certain He was anxious to teach us more. As I prayed, I felt assurance that things with the policy would somehow be okay, but I didn't think any changes would happen immediately.

Despite my best efforts and much study and prayer, I could not feel a spiritual confirmation of the November 2015 policy. And yet, I decided I could follow the counsel of President Dallin H. Oaks, who taught, "As part of my prayerful study, I learned that, in general, the Lord rarely gives reasons for the commandments and directions He gives to His servants. [But I have] determined to be loyal to our prophetic leaders."[1] I too was determined to remain loyal to prophetic leadership and to continue praying that God would send more light and knowledge just as He has always promised to do.

When President Nelson became the seventeenth President of the Church in January 2018, I felt uneasy. I had never quite gotten over what he had said as an Apostle at BYU–Hawaii two years before. As general conference approached a few months later, I still had unsettled questions. I needed a witness from the Holy Ghost. I needed to know that Heavenly Father was leading His Church and that the prophet and apostles were the men He had called, even if the November 2015 policy didn't feel right in my mind or in my heart.

I got in my car the Saturday morning of conference and drove to a church so I could participate in the solemn assembly with other Saints, but the church was closed. So I drove to another

---

1 "President Oaks Remarks at Worldwide Priesthood Celebration," June 1, 2018, newsroom.churchofjesuschrist.org.

one, and it was locked. And then another one, and it was locked, too. I had moved back to Provo the previous August, so there were many nearby churches to choose from. By this time I just needed to be somewhere to watch the meeting because it was about to start. So I returned home and watched the session on my laptop alone in my bedroom. When Melchizedek Priesthood holders were asked to stand, I stood up by myself in my room, dressed in a white shirt and tie, and raised my arm to the square to sustain a man that I was uneasy about. In that moment, a wave of the Spirit rushed over me. I felt in my whole body, but especially in my heart, that he had been called to lead at this time. I sat down and started to weep, grateful for the witness I had been given. And in an exceptionally cheesy moment, two tears landed on my knee and formed a heart shape on my pants.

The rest of the conference was soul-stirring, and President Nelson's multiple invitations to the members of the Church resonated deeply with me. I drove up to Salt Lake to attend the priesthood session that evening. When President Nelson instructed the brethren later that night to use the power of the priesthood to bless others I thought, *Yes! The power of God is here with us!* Then he invited all priesthood holders to literally rise up with him, and I felt a call to be better. I remember that when he entered the Conference Center for the priesthood session, everyone stood. Then everyone started to sit down as he sat down. Knowing this would happen, he faked everyone out and only pretended to sit and then stood back up. I thought, *This man is competent, confident, full of energy, and hilarious. This is my kind of prophet.* I had spent three months doubting his call, but now I no longer doubted because the Spirit testified to me that God had called President Nelson to lead the Church. Since that day, I have felt the Spirit testify of that truth again and again.

A year later, on April 4, 2019, I was sitting in class at BYU when the news broke that the Church had reversed the November 2015 policy. Children of same-sex couples could now be baptized, and homosexual immorality would be treated the same as heterosexual immorality. This news seemed to come out of nowhere, and I wasn't prepared to receive it. I didn't know what to do, so I stepped out of class and sat down in the hallway.

Two gay friends of mine ran by, late to give a presentation. "Did you hear, Ben?! Isn't it amazing?!"

"Yes! I heard! I just can't believe it!"

And off they ran. I sat in a busy hallway trying to take the news in, but I just couldn't wrap my head around it. I felt compelled to say a prayer of gratitude that my prayers of the past three and a half years had been answered. I wanted to cry to just let my emotions out, but tears didn't come.

When I returned to class, my teacher allowed me to tell everyone what had been announced. People were shocked and happy and congratulatory. There was joy in the room. I felt all those feelings, too. Then that night, as I was writing in my journal, I began to sob. The tears were triggered as I wrote about two events that happened earlier in the day.

After class, I sat and talked with some of my classmates about the announcement and what it meant to me. Candi, my fifty-eight-year-old, conservative classmate, gave me a long, long hug and said, "Ben, I want you to know how much I love you and admire you. You have taught me so much." And then another classmate gave me a hug and told me that the policy had been hard for her, too, and that she was glad we could start to move on. These moments were precious gifts from my friends.

During the three and a half years that the policy was in place, I feared being erased. What I needed to know was that I belonged. My classmates made it abundantly clear that I belonged in their lives, and not only that, but that they were grateful for my presence there. They literally and figuratively embraced me that day. As a gay, single, thirty-five-year-old member of the Church, I didn't always feel that I fit in, and my life certainly didn't look anything like I had thought it would. And yet, belonging is about far more than fitting in. To me, belonging means that the people in my life take me as I am, differences and all. That day I felt the people in my life say, "Ben, we claim you. You are one of us."

Five months later I walked into the BYU Marriott Center as a newly minted BYU employee to hear President Nelson speak. The title of his talk, "The Love and Laws of God," was displayed on huge screens long before he walked in. I immediately felt nervous. That phrase had previously been used to talk about LGBTQ issues, and I was worried about what President Nelson would say at this BYU devotional about people like me. When he walked into the room and everyone stood, I felt a wave of the Spirit just like the one I had felt when I sustained him. This was going to be okay.

Much of the talk really resonated with me. President Nelson spoke of how God gives us laws because He loves us. He taught that God's laws work every time. I've seen the fruits of living God's laws in my life and see how the principle of love helped to author them. President Nelson said the words *gay*, *lesbian*, and *LGBT* so many times throughout the talk. I was grateful that he chose to use those terms instead of "so-called gays and lesbians" or other dismissive phrases I had heard so often in the past. It was refreshing to hear the prophet use the term I use to describe myself. President Nelson invited us to seek our own confirmation that he and the other Apostles are God's prophets, and he shared that Church leaders saw the pain caused by the November 2015 policy and that they wept with us.

Towards the end of the talk, President Nelson said, "Though it may not have looked this way to some, the 2015 and 2019 policy adjustments on this matter were both motivated by love—the love of our Heavenly Father for His children and the love of the Brethren for those whom we serve." When Elder Christofferson said that the November 2015 policy was motivated by love, I couldn't believe him. It's not that I didn't want to believe—I just couldn't because it didn't feel right to me. Now, three and a half years later, the words rang true. I was able to believe it had all been done out of love. Like the Brethren, I have also done a lot of things in my life motivated by love that ended up causing pain to others. Being motivated by love doesn't always mean that the love is felt or received or immediately leads to the desired outcome.

Church has been hard at times. Trusting Church leaders has been difficult, even when their actions have been motivated by love. The words of Moroni resonate with me: "Condemn me not because of mine imperfection, neither my father, because of his imperfection, neither them who have written before him; but rather give thanks unto God that he hath made manifest unto you our imperfections, that ye may learn to be more wise than we have been" (Mormon 9:31). Moroni was imperfect. His father, Mormon, was imperfect. All the ancient American prophets before them were imperfect. I have learned that instead of criticizing or name calling, when I see things that feel like imperfections in the actions that the Church takes, I can pray for God to help me understand His will. Perhaps most important, I can try to do what Moroni says and be wise, learning from the imperfections of others.

Love is the greatest law. When things at church have been

hard or painful, it has never helped when someone tried to explain to me why I shouldn't be feeling pain. Invalidating hurt by giving explanations does not ease another's pain. What has helped are sincere expressions of love. Letting me know that I am loved and wanted and that I belong. Those kind gestures from my Latter-day Saint family have helped to ease my burdens and lessen the pain. Those have been beautiful, sacred moments. But what has really made the difference for me is being in places where the Spirit can talk to me. I have sought for and sometimes achieved a dialogic relationship with God in which I speak to Him and He speaks to me. I believe that my continued efforts to pray in faith and seek His guidance for me and my life have allowed Him to speak as I have prepared myself to hear. He has healed my hurt and, together with my fellow Saints, given me the strength I've needed to move forward.

PERFECTLY SINGLE

How do you find happiness as a single person?

When He comes, I so want to be caught living the gospel. I want to be surprised right in the act of spreading the faith and doing something good. I want the Savior to say to me: "Jeffrey, I recognize you not by your title but by your life, the way you are trying to live and the standards you are trying to defend. I see the integrity of your heart. I know you have tried to make things better first and foremost by being better yourself and then by declaring my word and defending my gospel to others in the most compassionate way you could."

–JEFFREY R. HOLLAND, "The Call to Be Christlike," *Ensign*, June 2014

The first time I met Georgina, she was shuffling out of her house in her favorite pink dress. Georgina was British, very honest, and super open about her life. The missionaries had asked me to give her a ride to church, and in those ten minutes I learned that she was anorexic, weighed seventy pounds, had two teenage children who didn't live with her, and that she hadn't been to church for a while. Georgina said that she didn't do much throughout the week and was lonely. I could tell she wanted a friend and thought maybe I could be that friend. I was living in Tucson and still had about two years left in my PhD program.

Since I was mostly working on my dissertation, my schedule was quite flexible. Before we got to church, I asked if I could take her to lunch that week. She readily accepted. I introduced her to many ward members and they immediately enveloped her, reaching out to this woman who had had a pretty tough life. Later that day she sent me a text that said in part: "I am feeling very happy. I was extremely scared of going to a new ward. I'm glad I finally took the plunge."

On Wednesday we went out to lunch. She talked and talked and talked. Since she spent most of her time alone, she relished the chance to have a listening ear. I recalled what my dad used to say when I would complain about a talk going long at church: "Sometimes just listening is the greatest gift you can give someone."

During that lunch she asked if I was a writer. "I write a lot for school," I said, "but I'm not really a writer." Georgina told me she believed she would die soon and had been wanting to write her life story. She asked me if I would do it. I told her I would. I mean, how could I say no? So the next week we got lunch again and I brought my laptop. After I ate, she told me stories and I typed them up. We did this week after week—her talking while I typed. She got emotional multiple times, and I experienced sacred moments as she pulled me into her treasured memories.

When I got home after that second lunch, I reflected on how crazy it was that I had three free hours in the middle of a Wednesday that I could dedicate to recording Georgina's story. I thought about my job and how I made enough money that I didn't even have to think twice about the expense of buying someone a meal at a nice restaurant. And I thought about how fortuitous it was that I randomly met this woman, and how being single had given me the opportunity to be her friend and make a record of her life. If I'd had a wife and children, I doubt I would have been able to do these things. But as a single thirty-two-year-old, I had time to do it.

Georgina and I got lunch every week for the next year and a half until I left Tucson. She loved seafood and Indian food more than anything, and occasionally she let me take her to my favorite Thai restaurant. When I came out to her at one lunch, the first thing she said was, "My initials spell G-A-Y, so I guess we have something in common."

Our relationship became deeply meaningful to me as we became constants in each other's lives. When I left on trips, she asked me to send her postcards so that she could experience those places through me. Months later I saw postcards from Niagara Falls, Prince Edward Island, New York City, Denmark, and other places I had been lovingly displayed on her wall. Neither Georgina nor I are very good singers, but every Sunday we would sit together at church and she would belt out the hymns. Those words couldn't have been sung more beautifully.

One fast Sunday after sacrament meeting, she said, "My heart has been pounding. I wanted to get up and say something, but I was too afraid."

"I know the feeling," I said. "You'll have the courage to get up next month." And she did. She was one of four friends who came to my graduation when I received my PhD. She had never been to an American graduation before and was so excited to go. She beamed with pride and was honored to meet my family. My friendship with Georgina was one of the most meaningful relationships I had while living in Tucson.

The commandment from God to Adam and Eve to "be fruitful, and multiply, and replenish the earth" (Genesis 1:28) is repeated in multiple temple ordinances. As a temple worker, I heard this phrase again and again and again. I pondered what it meant for me as a single person. I mulled over these words for weeks as I served in the temple. I initially thought that each of those phrases meant to have children—that God was commanding me to have children. Then I decided that God probably wouldn't use three different phrases to say the same thing. So I started to ponder each individual word and what it could mean to me, someone who has no biological children and most likely never will.

In His ministry, the Savior compared our works to fruit. Perhaps, I thought, I could keep the commandment to be fruitful by having and performing good works. The word *multiply*, I thought, maybe does just mean to have children. No huge insights with that one. A single person can't multiply. Then a friend pointed out that we're commanded to multiply and expand our talents. Maybe I could keep the commandment to multiply by actively working to increase my capabilities. Then I got stuck on the word *replenish*, because I didn't know what it meant.

When I got home one Tuesday night after working at the temple, I went to thesaurus.com to look up synonyms of *replenish*. Two of them really struck me: *renew* and *refresh*. I sat at my desk wondering, *What can I do to renew, refresh, and replenish the earth?* I thought, *Well, I could plant a tree or recycle.* But that felt a little shallow. As I thought about it more and more, it occurred to me that the earth was created for God's children, and if I wanted to renew, refresh, and replenish the earth, I needed to renew, refresh, and replenish God's children. This realization gave me a new daily goal: that everyone who interacted with me would feel renewed, refreshed, and replenished because of our time together. As Sheri L. Dew taught, "If we are going to build the kingdom of God, we as men and women of God must build each other" ("It Is Not Good for Man or Woman to Be Alone," *Ensign*, Nov. 2001).

I used to think that being single was a deficit, that there was something I was lacking. Now, however, I see that being single is a strength. It allows me to serve, renew, and refresh the world in ways that I couldn't if I were living the life I expected to have. If I were at home by myself watching Netflix all day, I'd be lonely and sad. But that's not how my life is at all. I am out and about doing good, trying to make the world a better place. Living life this way has helped me to be one of the least lonely people I know. Another benefit of being single is the freedom and the quiet. It is easy for me to find time to be alone and to ponder when I need it. I can easily shut out interruptions and be still. That is not a luxury that many of my married friends have.

Paul taught that God doesn't want all the members of the body of Christ to be the same. In 1 Corinthians 12:17–23, he explains that our differences strengthen the body of Christ. My grandma's old Bible was passed down to me after she died, and when I read those verses in a different translation, they jumped out at me a little more. "Suppose the whole body were an eye—then how would you hear? Or if your whole body were just one big ear, how could you smell anything? But that isn't the way God has made us. He has made many parts for our bodies and has put each part just where he wants it. What a strange thing a body would be if it had only one part! So he has made many parts, but still there is only one body. The eye can never say to the hand, 'I don't need you.' The head can't say to the feet, 'I don't need you.' And some of the parts that seem weakest and least impor-tant are really the most necessary. Yes, we are especially glad to have some parts that seem rather odd!" (*The Living Bible*, 1973; paraphrased). I have felt at times like I'm the odd part of the Church, like I don't really fit into the plan of happiness, but we are all necessary. Those of us who feel like it's best to stay single can build Zion in ways that other parts of the body can't.

Shortly after coming out in my early twenties, I sat with a friend and unloaded my fears about the future. "I just don't want to be alone forever," I worried. As I've gotten to know more and more LGBTQ Latter-day Saints, I hear this same story over and over again. While everyone's story is unique, this same sentiment has come up dozens and dozens of times: "I just don't want to be alone forever." The kind of people I hear say this are typically gay men who, like me, tried to date women for years with no success. They love the restored gospel and want to move forward in the Church, but doing so means that they either have to marry a woman or stay single. Since marriage to a woman is unappealing or doesn't work out, the only option left is to remain single if they want to fully participate in the Church. In their eyes, they will be alone forever. It is a heartbreaking prospect.

Our doctrine teaches that marriage is ordained of God, but beyond that, I just naturally want to be married. I want a partner who will be there with me through all the craziness of life. Sometimes words from the pulpit have made me feel like my life has less value because I am single. President Henry B. Eyring said that "everything we do should have celestial marriage as its focus and purpose" ("Eternal Families," *Ensign*, May 2016). And President Boyd K. Packer said, "The end of all activity in the Church is to see that a man and a woman with their children are happy at home, sealed together for time and for all eternity" ("The Plan of Happiness," *Ensign*, May 2015). I really love our doctrine on the eternal nature of families because I want to be with my family forever. I love my parents, siblings, sisters-in-law, nieces and nephews, and my extended family. They're just great. However, being taught that the whole point of activity in the

Church is marriage kind of stings for me as a very single person. That doesn't make the teaching less true, but it doesn't make it easy. And I've seen a lot of my female friends suffer greatly because they're single. Many tie their self-worth to marriage, and when marriage doesn't happen for them, it is absolutely devastating.

Ironically, people who oppose the Church's teachings on marriage have also encouraged me to find a spouse. A very well-intentioned woman once said to me, "It's too bad you're not dating, because I know some great guys I'd love to set you up with." I thanked her and told her that I was flattered she wanted to set me up with her friends. She then said, "We can chat again in a few years when you change your mind." I instantly felt defensive at her insinuation that my current life choices were just a phase. I get this a lot from people. A former professor of mine who is gay stumbled upon my blog a few years ago. He then sent me a Facebook message saying that reading my post filled him with sadness and encouraging me to find love now. He said, "Love is love, and practicing it is the greatest of God-given gifts." His message was incredibly kind, but he just couldn't understand my choice not to be in the kind of relationship I wanted.

I've talked to many people who have followed a similar path. They'll be told by members of the Church, "Marry a woman. It's part of God's plan for you." And then when that doesn't work, they try same-sex dating. Through it all they will worry and despair about being alone forever. My response to someone expressing this fear to me (hopefully after empathizing and validating that fear) is to say: "Just because you're single doesn't mean you have to be alone. You don't need a relationship to be happy. You're not half of a whole. You don't need another person to complete you." And then, in an effort to get a laugh while also saying something true, I'll say, "Feminism has taught me that I don't need a man to be happy."

I've said the phrase, "You're not half of a whole, you don't need another person to complete you," enough times that I decided to search the scriptures to see if it was true. I asked this question: What makes me whole and complete? The first scripture I explored was Matthew 5:48: "Be ye therefore perfect, even as your Father which is in heaven is perfect." From attending Sunday School I know that *perfect* means "complete, finished, fully developed." In other words, to be perfect is to be whole. The five verses preceding verse 48 all deal with how we treat other people. Verse 44, for example, says, "Love your enemies, bless them that curse you, do good to them that hate you, and pray for them which despitefully use you, and persecute you." As I've pondered these verses, I've understood them to mean that if I want to be whole, I need to forgive, I need to love, and I need to do good to everyone. In essence, my wholeness is contingent on how I treat other people. I become whole as I treat people as the Savior would.

I then found myself in Matthew 19:20–22, when a rich young man approaches Jesus and asks what he needs to do to receive eternal life. The Savior tells him to keep the commandments, to which the rich young man replies, "I keep all those commandments already." And then he asks, "What lack I yet?" In other words, what's keeping me from being whole? Christ tells him to give all he has to the poor, but the rich guy just can't do that. He walks away feeling sad and still incomplete. As I likened this verse to myself, I didn't feel that I was being asked to give all my stuff away (which really wouldn't take that long anyway). The message for me was deeper than that. I needed to ask, "What lack I yet? What am I missing?" and then have the courage to do that thing.

As I matured, I learned that I had to stop focusing on the outcome of marriage. I asked God, "What lack I yet?" and through a line-upon-line process, I came to know that there was a work

God had for me to do, and I felt prompted to reach out to other LGBTQ Latter-day Saints in Tucson. The scriptures are bursting with stories of how Christ treated everyone with love and respect, especially those that were sick, different, or on the fringes of society. Jesus showed us how love can be universal instead of exclusive. For me, the thing I lacked was reaching out to others. I was so focused on my own feelings that I had failed to realize that there were other lonely and sad people, too. None of us had to be alone, because we were meant to be family. I learned that I'm whole when I do God's will for me.

Even though I have many wonderful people in my life, sometimes I still feel the loss of a partner. I think that's normal and unavoidable. One day I was praying about that and wondering what I could do to form a deeper relationship. For months I'd been feeling a prompting to do something that had nothing to do with strengthening relationships, but I hadn't done it. As I prayed, I felt an impression that I would articulate as: "Ben, I already told you to do something, and you didn't do it. Do that thing and I'll let you know what the next step is." D&C 50:24 teaches, "That which is of God is light; and he that receiveth light, and continueth in God, receiveth more light; and that light growth brighter and brighter until the perfect day." I had received light that I hadn't acted on, and I would receive more light as I followed the promptings I'd already been given. I learned that I become whole as I receive more light.

There are a lot of great scriptures about what it means to be whole, but I'll just share one more thought. Moroni 10:32 says that "by his grace ye may be perfect in Christ." And, referring to those who will attain a celestial glory, D&C 76:69 says, "These are they who are just men [and women] made perfect through Jesus the mediator of the new covenant." In the end, it's not so much about what I do that will make me whole; it's about what

Christ did. A spouse won't complete me, but the grace of God will. The relationship that will make me perfect isn't the one I have with a significant other, but the one I have with Jesus. I am made whole through His grace.

If I could go back in time and sit with sad and lonely me, there are a few questions I would want younger Ben to consider: How do you treat other people? Is there something you feel prompted to do that you haven't had the courage to do yet? What are you doing to receive more light? What role does grace have in your life? I think if that younger Ben had really thought about it, he would have realized that he was looking for happiness in some of the wrong places. And then I would encourage him to follow the promptings of the Holy Ghost and his own moral compass and live the life he felt inspired to live. And I would tell him to not make any decisions based on fear (which is what I did for way too long).

I love traditional marriages and families and I believe that they are essential to God's plan. However, I do not feel called to pursue that kind of marriage. And while I'm very content with my life, I would not prescribe my life choices to any other LGBTQ Latter-day Saint. We all need to figure out what course is right for us. As Joseph Smith taught, "That which is wrong under one circumstance, may be, and often is, right under another. God said, 'Thou shalt not kill'; at another time he said, 'Thou shalt utterly destroy.' This is the principle on which the government of heaven is conducted, by revelation adapted to the circumstances in which the children of the Kingdom are placed. Whatever God requires is right, no matter what it is, although we may not see the reason thereof till long after the events transpire."[1] I feel that

---

1 "History, 1838–1856, volume D-1 [1 August 1842–1 July 1843] [addenda]," p. 3 [addenda], The Joseph Smith Papers, https://www.josephsmithpapers.org/paper-summary/history-1838-1856-volume-d-1-1-august-1842-1-july-1843/284.

I've received revelation on how to live my life, and I hope that everyone else will find their own guidance from God and follow the inspiration they receive.

I've heard many people say things like, "My wife is my rock," or "Nothing has brought me greater joy than raising my kids." These sentiments are great and no longer make me feel left out, because I've found my own rock and my own things that bring me joy. I know people who seem to have great marriages as well as people who feel burdened by their marriages. I also know people who are single and miserable and people who are single and thriving. That's because it's not our relationship status that completes us. It is who we are becoming that completes us.

One of the greatest lessons I have learned is that joy is available to me no matter my circumstances. As President Nelson taught, "The joy we feel has little to do with the circumstances of our lives and everything to do with the focus of our lives. When the focus of our lives is on God's plan of salvation . . . and Jesus Christ and His gospel, we can feel joy regardless of what is happening—or not happening—in our lives" ("Joy and Spiritual Survival," *Ensign*, Nov. 2016). And I would add, when the focus of our lives is on building Zion. I have always been active in the Church and have always strived to live Church standards, and yet for years I was miserable. What made all the difference for me wasn't necessarily changing *how* I lived the gospel but changing *why* I lived the gospel.

A year after I left Tucson, I got a call telling me that Georgina had died. I called her teenage son to see how he was doing, and he told me that as he went through her meager belongings, he found the printout of the stories that I had typed up for her. He thanked me for writing them, because it helped him to understand more about his mother's life. I was both grateful that I had taken the time to type out those stories and devastated that we hadn't recorded more. I had a dream that night that I was sitting in a restaurant with Georgina. I told her that she had died and that I needed to hear the rest of her life story so I could write it all down. But it was just a dream.

My journal also has stories from Georgina's life. I wrote about the time that I drove her to stake conference and she wept during one of the talks. Then she leaned over and said, "That talk was for me." I wrote about us going to the Tucson temple construction site and observing the progress of the building. I wrote about crying with Georgina as we both shouted "Hosanna!" at the Tucson temple dedication. I wrote about funny little instances like this one: "Tonight I walked outside to look at the sunset, and right as I was admiring the beauty in the sky I got a text from Georgina asking me to bring her food from Panda Express. My first thought was, 'I'm not a delivery service.' Then I realized that the beauty wasn't in the sky, but in the way I treat others. So I decided to get the food for her. Then as I was walking inside, I tripped over a bush."

Being single allowed me to be an active participant in Georgina's life. And my relationship with her helped me better understand the path to perfection and wholeness. As I shed the outcomes I had been looking for in life and focused on the outcome that really mattered—becoming like Jesus Christ—I found joy in the life that was designed for me.

LETTING PEOPLE IN

Why do you talk about your orientation at church?

Hooray for differences! Without them, there would be no harmony. In principles, great clarity. In practices, great charity.

–CHIEKO N. OKAZAKI, *Lighten Up* (Salt Lake City: Deseret Book), 1993

A few days after posting my coming-out blog post in January 2015, I was teaching elders quorum in my singles ward in Tucson. When I began the lesson I had no intention of telling my quorum that I was gay, but towards the end of the lesson I knew I had to. I awkwardly blurted out, "I'm gay," near the close of the lesson without much buildup. The unexpected way those words came out must've been jarring for some people in the room. I shared a few stories, ended the lesson, and sat down. A friend of the missionaries was attending church for the first time that day. He came up to me after and told me that he was part of the LGBTQ community and that my disclosure had helped him to feel more welcome. He had heard that members of the Church weren't very LGBTQ-friendly, and he was relieved to see that a gay person could be open about his sexuality and still be welcomed by the community. I initially thought that I had been prompted to come out to the quorum for this man's benefit, but I later realized that it was as much for me as it was for him.

More than a year later, a member of the bishopric who had been present at that lesson told me what he had witnessed. What he remembered most was watching me sit down. He said, "You looked lighter and more relaxed. You looked so relieved. It was evident in your body language that you felt a burden had been taken off your shoulders. Like you'd been holding your breath and could finally exhale." He got a little tenderhearted as he expressed how beautiful it was to see that healing take place in the quorum. I had been lying to people and hiding an important part of my life story from them, and it was such a relief to just be honest and open. I was finally letting my quorum in.

Not long after this lesson, I turned thirty-one and graduated from the singles ward without honors. I started attending a local Spanish branch and retreated back into the closet. It was awful. Members of the branch couldn't understand why I was single, and when they tried to set me up with their cousins, nieces, and friends, I would always say I was too busy with school to date. I hated not being fully transparent with them, but I didn't feel comfortable telling them the truth. I wanted to let them in but wasn't sure if they would be accepting.

That June, same-sex marriages became legal nationwide in the United States, and each Latter-day Saint congregation was asked to spend the third hour of a meeting in July reviewing some materials about marriage sent from Church headquarters. I had been home visiting my parents the first week in July and had had that lesson with my parents in their ward. The next week I was back in Tucson, and they had chosen that week for the marriage lesson. I almost went home after sacrament meeting because I didn't feel like having that lesson again, but I stayed. As I walked into the Relief Society room, I said a fervent, silent prayer. I told Heavenly Father that I wasn't planning to make any comments, but that if He wanted me to say something, He'd have to make it very clear.

About halfway through the meeting the branch president asked if there were any comments, and without me even realizing it, my hand shot up in the air. I said in Spanish, "This might be sharing too much information, but there are a lot of gay members of the Church who want to keep the commandments and stay active, and I'm one of them." I then talked about the need to love everyone and how the love and acceptance of family and friends had helped me to stay in the Church. Earlier in the meeting we had talked about "the gays" as if they were some group apart from us Latter-day Saints, but after my comment, the tone shifted. The rest of the meeting was great. The overarching theme was loving everyone as the Savior would. The branch president mentioned through tears that his daughter was a lesbian and had left the Church. He pointed to me and said that he loves me, and he loves us all. I felt enveloped by love. These people I barely knew felt like my family. As I let them in, they responded by wrapping their arms around me.

The branch president told everyone that I was his hero for being so open. That was not the reaction I had been expecting. At the end of the meeting we sang "Families Can Be Together Forever." I didn't always feel like I fit in in the Spanish branch, but as we sang that song, the Spirit spoke to my heart and told me that they were my family.

Four months later I started attending an English-speaking family ward. Not long after that, I was asked to give a talk about the purpose of the Church. Right before church I had a meeting with Bishop Adam Pershing. I assumed it was a get-to-know-you meeting, since I was new to the ward. He then surprised me by calling me to be ward mission leader. I asked Bishop Pershing if I could mention that I was gay in my talk. He replied, "I don't see why that would be a problem." I stood on the stand while a room full of strangers sustained me as the new ward mission leader for the Campbell Ward. I then walked to the pulpit and, with the permission of my bishop, told my new ward family that I was gay.

In the talk, I shared how difficult it had been at times to stay in the Church as someone who experiences same-sex attraction. I shared the story of Kevin and Allison's sealing and how that experience helped me to stay. After the meeting, about half a dozen people came up to me to introduce themselves and thank me for my talk. People I didn't know reached out to me and welcomed me into the ward. That afternoon, I got an email from a ward member I'd never met. He included his phone number and a picture of him and his wife so I would know who they were. He wrote: "I wanted to thank you for your words today in sacrament meeting. I admire your faith and courage. . . . I am glad to see your optimism, and your testimony has helped strengthen mine. You will not be forgotten if you stop coming to church. I will miss your presence. If you ever need to talk or hang out or just grab dinner, you are always invited into our home." I knew that I had found my home in the Campbell Ward.

One of the people who introduced herself to me after my talk was Vicki Allison. She told me that she was a ward missionary and was excited to work with me. I say this with no exaggeration: Vicki is one of the best ward missionaries in the Church. She and her husband open up their home to so many people. They love so sincerely. Vicki is very conservative and not the kind of person that I would have expected to have an openly gay friend, but she and I became buddies. One time I stopped by her house, and when I said I needed to go she hugged me and told me she loved me. Then two more times as she walked me out of the house she hugged me and said she loved me. One night I went to dinner with Vicki, her husband, and Bishop Pershing's family. As we laughed and chatted for two hours, I thought, *I could live in Tucson forever and have the best life.* Had they not known I was gay, there would have been this nagging feeling in my mind questioning if they would still want me in their lives if they knew. Since they knew me—all of me—I didn't have to wonder. Letting them into my life allowed me to feel love in a way that I couldn't if I'd continued to hide.

One of the people attending church the day I gave my talk was Taylor. It was his first time attending a Latter-day Saint meeting. Covered in tattoos and recently released from prison, he didn't know if he'd be welcomed in a Latter-day Saint congregation. Taylor later said that hearing my talk and then seeing the response I received after was the most powerful part of his conversion. He said, "Across the ward I saw nothing but nodding and smiles. The talk had everyone's attention, and without exception I saw love and acceptance. I was really looking, too. The hugs and handshakes tipped the scales for me. I, like many nonmembers, had some preconceived notions about how this church would treat its gay members socially. To see that our Church's high moral standards do not exclude loving, supporting, and giving equal respect to a gay member was a shock and such a wonderful surprise. I knew right then, at that moment, that this was the church for me."

The Campbell Ward in Tucson was Zion for me. It was the first place that I felt like I could just be me without having to pretend that I was something else. I didn't do it a lot, but when it felt right and came up organically, I mentioned being gay in lessons, talks, and individual conversations. Speaking at the BYU Religious Freedom Annual Review in 2018, Elder L. Whitney

Clayton said: "One cannot check religious identity at the church or synagogue exit or the door of one's home any more than one can check their race or ethnicity. Religious identity cannot be compartmentalized and stuffed into a box labeled 'private.'"[1] My orientation was something that I couldn't check at the door and stuff into a box either. I had tried doing that, and it made me miserable. Now that I was being more open and letting people in, I grew—and so did those around me.

The summer after moving to the Campbell Ward, I went on a road trip across the country. One Sunday I found myself in a small YSA branch of the Church in Iowa City. It was fast and testimony meeting, and there were only thirty of us present (I know because I counted). During the meeting, I just couldn't shake the feeling that someone there needed to know I was gay and needed to hear my testimony. So when there was a lull in the meeting, I stood up, walked to the pulpit, introduced myself, and came out to a roomful of strangers. Thanks to the good people of Tucson, I now had the courage and confidence to be me and share my faith as me. I talked about how life had been difficult at times, but how my friends and family had borne my burdens with me. I quoted Alma 33:23: "And then may God grant unto you that your burdens may be light, through the joy of his Son." I testified that that had happened for me in my life and shared how the Savior had lifted my burdens.

When church was over, a young woman came over to me and thanked me for my testimony. She told me that she had a friend who's a lesbian who was struggling with her faith, and she wanted to know how to help her. I told her that she needed to love her friend and be with her on her journey. She and I then exchanged

---

1 In Tad Walch, "LDS leader insists religious identity deserves same protections going to sexual, gender identities," *Deseret News*, June 20, 2018.

email addresses, and I was grateful that I had found the one person out of twenty-nine who needed to talk to me.

After church I said goodbye to the few people I had talked to there and walked out the door. As soon as I was outside, one of the guys I'd met slid out the door right behind me. He thanked me for my testimony and told me that he had been so emotional during the meeting that he'd had to leave the room. He told me that he also experienced same-sex attraction, that it had been so hard, and that he hadn't wanted to come to church that day. I listened to his story and shared some encouraging words. I told him what I tell all of my gay Latter-day Saint friends: "You are not alone. We're going to do this together."

I exchanged email addresses with this man and emailed him a few days later just to see how he was doing. Part of the email reply said, "Thank you for reminding me that I don't have to do this alone." Alma taught his people to have "their hearts knit together in unity and in love one towards another." As they did this, "they became the children of God" (Mosiah 18:21–22). To me that's one of the main points of the gospel—that we're all brothers and sisters. As we knit our hearts together, we become more like God. But we can't unite our hearts if we don't let each other in. And we can't become who God wants His children to be if we don't receive the gift of vulnerability when it is offered to us.

As I opened up to people in my ward and let them in, they started letting me in, too. I became a reservoir for stories that members of my ward family couldn't share with anyone else. I heard about gay friends, and transgender cousins, and bisexual in-laws. And I heard about a lot of LGBTQ children. One older friend of mine pulled me aside one day because he said he had a question. He told me he had a gay son who was married to his husband. He was very clear that he loved his son and son-in-law and that they were both integral parts of the family. Then he got teary-eyed and asked so sincerely, "How do I make sure my son knows how much I love him?" I don't remember what I said, probably because in that moment he didn't need *me* to say anything. There was something that he needed to hear himself say. As he cried, he said, "I know that God loves my son so much. Because I love him so imperfectly and I love him so much. I can't imagine what God's perfect love looks like, but it must be powerful if it's stronger than my love for him." His own testimony of God's love for his son was what he needed that day, and I didn't have to do anything. I was just the lucky one who happened to be witness to that beautiful moment.

When I moved from Tucson to Provo in 2017, I wasn't sure how open I could be with my new ward. I had been warned by a few people that Church members in Utah would not be as kind to me as Church members in Tucson had been. I was advised to go back in the closet. I moved into an apartment with two random BYU students. My second day there, one of them mentioned having a woman over earlier in the day. My natural reaction would be to immediately pry and ask, "Are you in love with her? Did you kiss her?" But if I turned the conversation towards dating then he might ask me about my dating life. If that happened, should I avoid the topic or come out to him? And what if he felt uncomfortable living with a gay guy? What would I do then? I decided to steer the conversation away from dating to avoid any awkwardness. I was afraid of how coming out might affect this new friendship, and that was a fear I hadn't felt for a long time.

Then at church on Sunday, I was filling out one of those get-to-know-you forms for new members. The last question on the form was: Is there anything you'd like us to know about you? Here I was, in a brand-new ward, where I only knew one person, in a super conservative place in the heart of Provo, Utah. I hesitated for a moment, thinking it might be best to not disclose my sexual orientation so early, before people got to know me. My mind flashed back to the night before, when I had attended the LoveLoud festival in Orem. The Church had endorsed the event, and it was packed with all kinds of people. I had felt so at home. In between each of the musical performances, they had people come to the stage to share messages. Carol Lynn Pearson recited a poem she had written for the event about how a butterfly cannot return to its chrysalis. As I looked at the new-member form, I considered what Carol Lynn Pearson's poem meant for me. Then I scribbled the words "I'm gay" on the form.

After the meeting, two members of the Welcoming Committee came over to talk to me. I knew they hadn't seen the form yet, so I considered playing straight so they wouldn't feel uncomfortable, but they asked about why I was in Provo. I told them honestly that I was starting a master's in social work so that I could become a therapist and work with LGBTQ Latter-day Saints. They asked me what led me to want to do that, and I told them I was gay. They both responded really well, and one of them had even attended LoveLoud the night before and had loved it. He said it would be so great to have an out gay person at church. The other person said she was happy to have me in the ward and asked if she could take me to lunch to ask me a few questions. I was glad I hadn't hidden.

After church I met with my bishop, J. B. Haws. I momentarily considered withholding my orientation so that he could get to know me first, but I ended up coming out to him anyway. He responded in the best possible way. He asked some great questions, and I told him about my blog and the things I'd been doing in Tucson. He pulled up my blog on his laptop right then and said he'd read it. My main worry about coming out to my bishop was that he wouldn't want to recommend a gay man to be a temple worker. So when I expressed interest in being a temple worker and he said, "I would feel 100% comfortable recommending you as a temple worker," I was over the moon.

We didn't have a lot of time to chat because he had other interviews after me, but he asked if he could take me out to lunch so we could chat more. I replied, "Of course! Free lunch to talk about LGBTQ stuff is my favorite thing!"

Bishop Haws then said, "I have one last question. What do you need me to know and understand so that I can serve you better?" I was touched by that beautiful, sincere question. In the few minutes we spoke, it was evident that my new bishop was sincerely trying to serve in a Christlike way. He didn't offer any counsel; he just listened, learned, and empathized. I walked out of the church building a few minutes later invigorated by the Spirit and stunned that things had gone so well. I got in my car and literally shouted for joy and said a prayer of thanksgiving as I drove away. I just couldn't believe that it had gone so well. I have enjoyed many lunches with Bishop Haws since that day we first met.

Leaving Tucson was a scary decision for me. It was my home and the first place I was able to be me. I remember sitting in the Tucson temple three days after it was dedicated and having an overwhelming feeling that I was among my people. A few days later I moved to Utah. My second day in Utah, at the LoveLoud Festival in Orem, I had the same feeling—that I was with my people. I felt that same Spirit again as I left my new church building that first Sunday. I now understand that for me to feel like I belong, the people around me have to really know me. And for that to happen, I need to have the courage to let them in, and they need to accept that invitation.

I've visited Tucson many times since I moved away in August 2017. My days there are spent visiting people, because there are so many people that I want to see. During these visits, I often thank the people who had such an enormous impact on my life. For example, Brother Bauer, the institute director who was the first person to invite me to share my story publicly. President Walker, who supported me in my desire to start a support group for LGBTQ Latter-day Saints in the area. Bishop Pershing, who gave me permission to come out to the ward and be me. Each of these people took time to get to know me and my story, and to see my heart. Each of them used their positions in a way that gave me courage and helped me to feel comfortable as a gay Latter-day Saint. Each of them could have easily and politely said no and clipped my wings, but instead they let me soar. I talk about Tucson and how much I love it probably a little too much. Someone asked me once why I have such an affinity for the city. I said, "Because some of the finest people I have ever met call Tucson home, and it's the first place that I was able to me."

A VIEW FROM THE MARGINS

What have you learned as a gay man in a straight community?

On those days when we feel a little out of tune, a little less than what we think we see or hear in others, I would ask us . . . to remember it is by divine design that not all the voices in God's choir are the same. It takes variety—sopranos and altos, baritones and basses—to make rich music. To borrow a line quoted in the cheery correspondence of two remarkable Latter-day Saint women, "All God's critters got a place in the choir."
-JEFFREY R. HOLLAND, "Songs Sung and Unsung," *Ensign,* May 2017

During my time as a doctoral student at the University of Arizona, I regularly taught introductory Spanish classes. I told my class one day that we would be ending early because I had an appointment. Someone asked where I was going. "An interview." Someone else asked what the interview was for. "It's an interview for a documentary." Another student asked what the documentary was about. "It's about gay Mormons." Another student slapped his hand on his desk in shock and blurted out, "You're Mormon?!"

I had told all my students that I had attended BYU, and since this was a Spanish class, they all knew that I had spent two years as a missionary in Mexico. I thought it was pretty obvious from connecting the dots that I was a Latter-day Saint, but at least this one student hadn't gotten the memo. I was surprised that what was shocking to him wasn't my sexual orientation but my religious affiliation.

I experience a lot of privileges. I'm a tall, white, educated, male with hair. And yet, I'm part of two minority groups. I'm a sexual minority, and (when I live outside of Utah) I'm a religious minority. These two aspects of my identity can be easily hidden or downplayed. If someone were to see me as just a white male, or just a gay man, or just a Latter-day Saint, they would miss out on the complexities that shape who I am. One of the pitfalls of stereotypes is that we oversimplify who others can or can't be because of our image of who belongs in which category. As someone who is mostly in the majority and only a little bit of a minority, I've been able to experience just a small portion of what it's like to be on the margins.

My non-Latter-day-Saint friends and family tend to be pretty unfazed when I come out to them. For example, I became fast friends with Laura, a classmate of mine at the University of Arizona. She later earned the nickname "Fun Laura" because she's a total blast. As we started to hang out away from school events, I invited her to go to the Gilbert Arizona Temple open house with me. Shortly after I picked her up, I told her that I was gay. This was a weighty, important disclosure for me. Her response was basically, "Yeah? And?" She really didn't care. Not only did this information not surprise her, but she had no emotional reaction to my coming out. It was just a new fact, and a rather uninteresting one at that. This was quite different from the reactions of my Latter-day Saint friends, who often got these confused looks on their faces that seemed to say, *How can this be?* Laura was kind enough a few weeks later to let me spill my guts and tell her my entire gay Latter-day Saint journey. I'm sure she found parts of it to be rather peculiar.

A year and a half later, I was looking for a new place to live near the University of Arizona. Laura had seen an ad from two women who were renting a room in their house. The ad said that they were looking for a female international student. Laura forwarded me the ad and said the place was perfect for me. I didn't think they'd want me living in their house, because I was most certainly not a female international student. But I wrote them an email explaining that I had lived abroad a ton and that I was a Latter-day Saint so I didn't drink, smoke, swear, or party. I also told them that I was gay and was very accepting of other lifestyles. They invited me over, we clicked right away, and they invited me to rent the room (which was a steal of a deal). A few weeks later, I moved into a beautiful little home with two retired lesbians (they were retired professionally, not from being lesbians).

After we had gotten to know each other, the homeowner asked me how I could be part of the LDS Church as a gay person. She sincerely wanted to understand my choice to be in a church that didn't seem to want people like me. I basically shared my testimony with her and told her how the Book of Mormon had changed my life. She had read the Book of Mormon when she was a teenager, so she had some context for what I was saying. However, my testimony didn't seem to satisfy her desire to know why I would attend this church when there were so many churches that would allow me to be in a same-sex relationship. Then I said, "I want my congregation to be the best, most welcoming place it can be. If you and your partner ever want to come to church, there is always room for you on the pew next to me." I told her that my commitment to the Church wasn't just because it made me better, but because I wanted to make it better, too. That answer was much more satisfying to her.

I lived with these two women when the November 2015 policy became international news. One of them stuck her head into my room one day to ask me what the heck was going on in my church. She was baffled by it, and I tried my best to explain, but it hadn't made much sense to me either. She was trying to understand—how could a gay person possibly be part of this church? I told her again that I was committed to making my congregation the very best place that it could be. Not long after this, Ally Nights started—in their living room. They witnessed dozens and dozens of people come to their home to better understand the LGBTQ Latter-day Saint experience. I don't know if they ever fully understood why I was choosing to be a Latter-day Saint, but they respected me and my friends. They didn't keep me on the margins of their lives. In fact, they bragged about me to their friends—their gay Mormon roommate who was making his church a better place. They became my family.

As an active Latter-day Saint, I don't really fit into the LGBTQ world. And as a gay person, I don't often fit into the Latter-day Saint world. As someone who could so easily be forgotten and marginalized, I am so grateful for those in the majority who actively try to listen to and understand the minority. They are the ones who leave the ninety and nine to be with the one.

When I returned to BYU in 2017 to pursue a master's in social work, my minority status shifted. Now it wasn't weird that I was a Latter-day Saint; it was weird that I was gay. I worked as an adjunct Spanish professor my first year back and wasn't sure if I was allowed to come out to my students. On the first day of classes a student asked about my family, and I quickly changed the subject. Later in the semester I had to miss class to represent

BYU at an LGBTQ conference hosted by the NCAA. I hadn't told my students why I would be missing class, but when I got back I knew I had to tell them. I was so nervous and probably a little awkward as I explained to my students that I had been asked to represent LGBTQ BYU students at a conference. My students were so kind, and they asked some good questions. In the days that followed, I waited for a report that someone had complained about me coming out to my class, but no report ever came. My orientation came up a few more times during the semester and I shared some brief stories. When I read my student reviews after the semester was over, half of the comments mentioned how much they appreciated that I had come out to the class and what an important experience that had been. It had been a meaningful experience for me, and I was touched that it was meaningful for them as well.

The next semester I came out to my class much earlier. I showed them a picture of Fun Laura as part of a story, and someone asked me if I was in love with her and was going to marry her. I said, "There are at least three reasons why I won't be dating Laura." Someone then asked what those reasons were. "Well," I said, "she lives in a different state, we have different religious beliefs, and I'm not attracted to women." The entire class seemed to gasp at once. That is not what they were expecting me to say. That's what it can feel like on the margins—that my very existence is shocking to people. Once again, though, my students were so good. They were grateful that we were able to have that conversation.

I have learned that not all people on the margins have the same experience. Shortly after returning to BYU in 2017, I was asked to be part of a committee comprised of a number of campus administrators and nine LGBTQ students. While my experience at BYU had been overwhelmingly positive, that was not the case for other students. During one particularly charged meeting, an LGBTQ student was expressing his hurt and frustration at a decision that had been made. My initial impulse was to defend and explain the decision. Luckily, before I could say anything, another LGBTQ student jumped in and said, "I'm so sorry you've been so hurt, and that makes me hurt." It was exactly the right thing to say. Her validation of his experience feeling marginalized eased the tension, and as a group we were able to move forward. During this meeting, the administrator in charge, Steve Sandberg, showed us a picture his six-year-old daughter drew that day that included a rainbow. She said she drew it because she knew some of daddy's friends loved rainbows and because they make her happy.

One of the things we planned as a group was a campus-wide LGBTQ & SSA panel. On the panel we had an L, a G, a B, and a T. I was honored to be the G. A few days before the panel, I mentioned to an administrator friend of mine that someone from the area had been harassing me online. He told me that he would be watching out for that person and would make sure that the other panelists and I were protected. He said that he would not tolerate any guff from anyone who attended. Sharing my story openly with more than a thousand people at BYU was a scary thing to do, and it was comforting to know that those in the administration were looking out for us. The panel happened in part because non-LGBTQ administrators insisted that our voices needed to be heard.

Many beautiful stories were shared during the ninety-minute panel. One of the panelists talked about opening up to his mission companion about what he was experiencing. His companion responded by saying, "You know, we're walking on holy ground." The whole panel experience felt like being on holy ground. We were all vulnerable, honest, and hopeful as we answered questions from the audience, not mincing words as we discussed tough experiences. Then, as the panel ended, the completely packed auditorium burst into applause and a sincere standing ovation. As I watched hundreds of people rise from their seats, my eyes welled with tears at this spontaneous gesture. Never in a million years did I think I'd be able to openly share my story at BYU and then be applauded for it.

As I discussed this moment later with my straight friends, some of them explained what it felt like to be in the audience applauding. They said that they applauded the panelists because of our courage to openly share our stories. They were validating our life experiences and our engagement with faith, belief, love, acceptance, and contradiction. They were celebrating us because of the courage it takes to not give up or feel bitter while reconciling our faith and our unique circumstances.

While I was waiting my turn to answer the last question on the panel, I got a strong impression to tell the audience that this event wouldn't have happened without the support and help of administrators at BYU. Then I totally forgot to mention them in my closing remarks. As the last two panelists spoke, I felt a pit in my stomach knowing that I had missed an important prompting. As one of the moderators was sharing her final thoughts, Sarah, another panelist, leaned over to me and said, "I feel like we need to say something about the work the administrators have done to make this happen."

Incredibly relieved, I said, "I just felt the exact same prompting!"

Sarah replied with a wink, "By the mouth of two or three witnesses."

As soon as the moderator finished speaking, Sarah turned on

her mic and explained to the room, "I felt really compelled to say this. I need everyone in this room to know that the moderators are just a small sample of the administration, faculty, and staff here at BYU that are doing everything they can to make this a better place for the LGBTQ students here at BYU. I am a witness that there are people here advocating for you at every level of this university and that you can trust them. And I just wanted to say thank you publicly." That was the message the Holy Ghost wanted everyone present to hear, and I'm thankful that Sarah had the courage to be the messenger.

In one of the last moments of the event, one of the moderators asked anyone in the room who identified as LGBTQ or same-sex attracted, and who felt comfortable doing so, to stand. Probably about a fifth of the room stood, and the audience erupted into applause. I nearly burst into tears watching my straight peers clap for my LGBTQ family. The moderator was quoted in the *Salt Lake Tribune* as saying, "LGBT and [same-sex-attracted] students don't only exist at BYU, they belong at BYU." I felt much less on the margins that evening.

Three months later, in June 2018, I was asked to be on a panel titled "Fostering Faith and Community at BYU with LGBTQ Students" as part of the BYU Religious Freedom Annual Review. I represented the LGBTQ student population at BYU. The other panelists were an LGBTQ activist from the community and two BYU administrators, Steve Sandberg and Julie Franklin. During the Q&A, an audience member asked a question that turned into a very long comment. He said that we all know that in the next life, everyone will have the correct attractions to the opposite gender and wanted to know what we were doing to make sure that everyone understood this truth. I was sitting next to Steve, who knows me very well, and who knew that this particular question would be triggering for me. As the man continued to speak, Steve's hand rested on my knee. He gave it a gentle squeeze, which I took to mean, *I got you. I'm here with you.*

When the man was done talking, Steve took the initiative to answer the question so I wouldn't have to. It was an incredibly kind thing for him to do and made me feel protected. However, I knew I had to speak, too. When Steve was done, I leaned towards my mic and explained that this question was a particularly tough one for me because I had been taught exactly what this man was lobbying for us to teach. I told him that for me, being taught that I would be straight in the next life was dangerous and unproductive because it just made me want to be dead so that I could get to that next life. Then I quoted 1 John 3:2, 1 Corinthians 2:9, and Doctrine and Covenants 58:3. I explained that instead of focusing on what my orientation will be like, I try to focus on becoming like Jesus Christ.

As administrators, Steve and Julie spent countless hours listening to the stories of LGBTQ students. This was outside of their already busy schedules. They listened and learned because they truly cared. They left their ninety and nine work responsibilities to be with the one. Julie became emotional as she said, "I became a better person as I got to know LGBTQ BYU students. As I began to see them and love them the way God sees and loves them, I was better able to see myself the way God sees me, too." They had heard the stories of students who felt marginalized, and those stories had changed them.

When the session was over, Steve gave me a big hug and told me that he loved me. A few people came up and apologized for the man's insensitive question. I told them that I was glad he had asked it so that I could share my perspective and teach truth. His question had given me the opportunity to testify of the Savior. I was grateful that Steve had been there next to me—not only to stand up for me with his words, but because I felt safe knowing that he had my back.

What I've noticed as a person on the margins is that others sometimes want to dismiss or minimize my experiences. People who are not members of the Church tell me that I should just leave my religion. To them it's that simple. Once they understand me and my story, though, they see the complexities of the choices I'm making. That takes some hard work. It takes looking beyond the stereotype of what they think a Latter-day Saint is and really getting to know me and the nuances of my life goals. I also find that too many people in the Church are eager to explain away the complexities of being a gay Latter-day Saint, preferring a simple explanation over the hard work of overlaying the ideal with the real. I have a lot of experience with that reaction, and I see it happening to other people as well.

For example, my sister is two years older than me and she's never been married. The pressure to get married coupled with seeing friend after friend get married has been tough on her. Lindsay has regularly been told that it's okay if she doesn't get married in this life because she'll have the opportunity in the next life. I believe that this is true and could provide comfort, but it discounts the pain and loneliness she might be feeling now. Imagine seeing a family crying at the airport after just dropping off their daughter for her mission. I wouldn't say, "Don't be sad, she'll be home in eighteen months. An eternal perspective will make all the sadness of you missing her right now go away." Telling people not to feel their feelings rarely comforts or lifts—even with a sound doctrinal explanation. Healing comes more readily when we invite others to share their feelings and then listen and love them as they do.

My natural response used to be to minimize the hurt that

others feel. I believe that came from me not understanding what it was like to feel different or excluded. As I began to see the ways that I felt marginalized, I became more compassionate. One day I got a call from a single friend in her mid-thirties. When I asked how she was doing, she burst into tears and said, "How do you do it? How are you happy single? I'm so lonely." I had learned that even though she was asking me a question, she didn't need answers from me. She just needed me to be with her.

LGBTQ folks and unmarried people aren't the only members of the Church who feel marginalized at times. Feeling left out or out of place is a common experience. As Elder Holland empathetically stated: "There is room for those who speak different languages, celebrate diverse cultures, and live in a host of locations. There is room for the single, for the married, for large families, and for the childless. There is room for those who once had questions regarding their faith and room for those who still do. There is room for those with differing sexual attractions" ("Songs Sung and Unsung," *Ensign*, May 2017). My view from the margins has helped me to see that the Savior cares about the one. It has also helped me to see that there is room for all kinds of people in the Church of Jesus Christ. And part of my duty as a covenant member of the Church is to make sure that those around me are seen and know that they belong.

THE FAMILY OF GOD

How do you deal with the loss of the life you thought you'd have?

Being a good sibling, daughter, granddaughter, and aunt are not throwaway roles. They are sacred.

–SHARON EUBANK, "A Letter to a Single Sister," *Ensign*, Oct. 2019

When I was twenty-nine, I worked part-time as a release-time seminary teacher in Tucson. Teaching seminary had always been a dream of mine. On the long drive home from teaching, I often offered prayers of gratitude for the privilege of working with such remarkable youth every day. While gratitude was the norm, one day I left feeling really down. I don't recall the content of the lesson, but the reality of my perpetual singleness was weighing on me more than usual. That day, during the forty-minute drive across town back to my house, I poured out my heart to God. Hadn't God promised me a family of my own? Hadn't He promised me posterity? I prayed out loud as I drove, begging, "Heavenly Father, why can't I have a family?"

As I pulled into my driveway, I felt a clear impression: "Ben, you already have a family."

I have parents and siblings and nieces and nephews who love me and care about me. I was so focused on the family I didn't have that I had failed to be appropriately grateful for the family

I did have. As Elder Neal A. Maxwell taught, "Yearning for expanded opportunities while failing to use those at hand is bad form spiritually" ("Content with the Things Allotted unto Us," *Ensign*, May 2000). After this experience I made more of an effort to connect with my family. Since I was a few states away from my immediate family, I started calling my parents more often instead of just my weekly Sunday call. I reached out to my siblings more and tried to be an active participant in their lives.

A word of caution: I would not recommend telling people who are single that they already have a family so they shouldn't be sad or mourn the loss of the family they wish they had. That kind of intended comfort would not have felt comforting to me. Like most of the truths that have changed my life, this one came through the Holy Ghost. I believe that He is the only Being that could communicate that knowledge to me in a way that would sink into my soul. I know that my roles as a brother, uncle, and son are important and sacred, but they don't fully erase the loss I feel in my other missing roles. One of the principal ways that I have been comforted is to be in a place where the Holy Ghost can teach me truth.

I have had a lot of tough moments as I've mourned the loss of the life I thought I would have. My parents went through their own grieving process as they came to understand that my life would not be what they had expected. More than a decade after coming out to them, I asked my dad what was hard for him about accepting our new normal. He said, "I was sad that you would never get to be a dad, because you would be such a great dad." I then asked him how he got over that grief. He said, "I never did get over that." His response surprised me. I assumed he had long since moved on. In that same conversation, he talked about all the great things I was doing and how proud he was of me, but his grief over that loss still remained. And I think that's okay. I don't think it would be fair for me to expect that his loss of the future he thought his son would have is something that he would just "get over." It's something I never have really gotten over either.

When I was doing my master's in social work at BYU in 2018, we had a class in which we talked about being present with our feelings. One Sunday I went on a walk and ended up at the Provo City Center Temple. As I walked around the grounds that summer Sunday afternoon, I listened to sacred music and tried to really connect with how I was feeling. I wrote in my journal that evening, "I sat outside the temple and saw so many couples holding hands. Usually I would tell myself that I'm doing well single, and I am, but it was also painful." It hurt that I didn't have a partner. It hurt that I wasn't able to be in a relationship. It hurt that I was on a walk by myself when I would have rather been walking with my companion. This is more than simply comparing my life to other people's lives. This isn't me feeling sad because someone has something that I don't. This is sadness over a dream and a need unmet. I think everyone can relate to that sorrow.

I don't believe that there is anything someone could say when I'm feeling that kind of sadness that would make it go away, but there is plenty that someone could do. In moments like this, particularly astute friends have reached out before I have even asked for help. This happened years ago, before I had come out publicly. On one particularly tough evening, my friend LeAnne called. She had no idea that I'd been feeling down and that I desperately needed to talk to someone. My roommate didn't know I was gay and I didn't want him to overhear our conversation, so I stepped out of the house, walked down the road, and sat on a curb by a park.

During our ninety-minute conversation, I told LeAnne that

I had a crush on a boy in my ward. This was one of the very first times I had admitted to another person that I liked a guy and said his name. She didn't judge me, reprimand me, or try to solve my problems; she just listened and encouraged me. I told her how hard it was to have to choose between being in the Church and being with someone I was attracted to. I asked why I have to choose between the gospel and companionship when other people don't have to. LeAnne didn't have an answer, so she just listened and cried with me. I shared my favorite line from *Preach My Gospel* with her: "All that is unfair about life can be made right through the Atonement of Jesus Christ."[1] She testified that she knew that was true. I said, "I know it's true, too." I have learned that I rarely need someone to tell me something comforting. What I need is for them to help me say that thing for myself. LeAnne wasn't the one who shared the inspiration I needed; I shared it. Her patience and good listening helped me be in a place where I could express the truth that I needed to hear.

The shortest verse in all of our scriptures simply says, "Jesus wept" (John 11:35). He cried because Mary had just told Him that her brother Lazarus had died. And even though Lazarus would soon be raised from the dead and all would be well, Jesus shared in Mary's pain and wept with her. I have often felt awkward when someone cries around me, but when LeAnne cried with me it felt like a gift. She was feeling my pain, sharing my burden, and empathizing with me in a very real way. She wept with me, just as the Savior would have had He been with me.

Those are special moments when I know not only that my friends care but that God cared enough to prompt them to reach out. More often than not, I need to reach out when I'm in those

---

1 *Preach My Gospel: A Guide to Missionary Service* (Salt Lake City: The Church of Jesus Christ of Latter-day Saints, 2004), 52.

moments. Usually I just need someone who will listen to me for a few minutes and then we can move on to other things. Sometimes I'll call a friend and say, "I'm feeling sad and I just need to talk about it." And they will listen.

As I've pondered about my lack of my own spouse and children, I've come to see that family is a much larger concept than I had allowed myself to see when I was myopically focused on marriage. As children of God, we are all part of God's family. As members of the restored Church, we are part of a covenant family. Groups of people form themselves into found families. And, of course, we have our biological and legal families. I am a part of many families, and that has helped to lessen the pain of not having my own biological family.

I haven't had a girlfriend since I dated Becca in 2010. I haven't mentioned her previously because I've already shared plenty of dating stories. At the time, I really thought we would eventually get married, and I got to know her family well. Years later her dad invited me to give a fireside in their stake in Atlanta, Georgia. I spent a weekend in February 2018 with Becca's parents and two youngest siblings. I had such a wonderful time. However, it was odd to be in Becca's house without her. It was odd to sleep in the guest bedroom that I thought I would be sleeping in when we visited for Christmas and other holidays. And it was odd to spend the weekend with people who I thought would be my in-laws someday and weren't. After the fireside, I drove back to Becca's parents' house with her dad and siblings. Since I had just spilled my guts to a room full of strangers, I continued spilling my guts in the car. I told them how years before I had thought that we would be family. Becca's youngest sister then said, "Ben, you are our family."

The Lord, through Isaiah, spoke to two groups of people in

Isaiah 56 that often grieve in Zion. One of those groups was the eunuchs—male Church members who couldn't have children. The Lord told them not to call themselves "dry trees" because while they couldn't reproduce, they could still be productive. He tells them to do three things: keep the Sabbath, do the things that please God, and make covenants with Him. And then He gives these childless Church members a promise: "Even unto them will I give in mine house and within my walls a place and a name better than of sons and of daughters: I will give them an everlasting name, that shall not be cut off" (Isaiah 56:5). It is a beautiful, eternal truth that we are all children of God. And yet, God has called us to be more than His children. In the temple He gives us a higher calling. He promises the childless an everlasting inheritance with Him.

In August 2018 I moved into Charlotte's basement. At the time, she was eighty-five years old and had been a widow for seventeen years. She and I became fast friends as we shared meals together, raked leaves, and discussed current events. Every evening when I got home, Charlotte and I would sit and talk for at least twenty minutes. That was often the best part of my day. One day I came home and Charlotte told me she had been crying. It was the anniversary of her husband's passing. We sat and talked and she told me stories about him. There really wasn't anything I could do to help but to be there with her.

One Sunday, Charlotte asked me how the new *Come, Follow Me* program worked. I told her that there was a block of scriptures that Church members were supposed to study at home each week with their families. She asked, "Well what if you don't live with your family?" I said I didn't live with my family either, so we could do the reading together. Most nights we would sit at the kitchen table and read from the scriptures. Often I would have friends over who would read with us. Serious discussions of doctrine were often punctuated by laughter. I read aloud, "Ye adulterers and adulteresses" (James 4:4), and Charlotte interrupted dryly, "Oh good, some gender-inclusive language." One night after reading the scriptures with Charlotte and a friend, I wrote in my journal: "Everything in my life feels good right now. Not for any particular reason. I just feel so good and so grateful."

I remember my heart warming the first time Charlotte referred to us as a family. Whenever I would come home from a trip we would sit down and she'd catch me up on whatever I had missed. She always told me how glad she was that I was back and that she had missed me. It was nice to come home to someone who felt like family every night. It was nice to read the scriptures together. And it was nice to have someone around who never hesitated to tease me. I'm sure Charlotte would much rather have had her husband to read the scriptures with than me. I would have rather had a spouse as well. But instead we had each other. And our quirky little family was a beautiful addition to my life.

One day we were reading King Benjamin's sermon. I paused after we read Mosiah 3:13. I pointed out that the people were able to "rejoice with exceedingly great joy, even as though [Christ] had already come among them." What an interesting idea, I pondered, rejoicing in something that hasn't happened yet. I looked up at Charlotte and said that even though her husband wasn't physically present, she knew that someday she'd be with him again. I don't know what my future holds, but I do believe that at some future day I'll have a spouse. I don't think it's wise to live in the future. I want to live in the here and now. And yet, I want to be able to rejoice in an outcome that hasn't happened, but will most certainly happen. I don't quite know what it looks like to rejoice in a future spouse, but I try to trust in God and His promises. And as I reflect on the promises that God has made to all His children, and to me in particular, I have many reasons to rejoice.

Widows and gay men aren't the only people whose circumstances are different than they would choose. One of these people is my friend Melanie. I can say with absolutely no hyperbole that Melanie is one of the best people I know. She has a heart of gold and loves and cares about others so sincerely. I met her in 2017 when she was asked to be one of the LGBTQ outreach coordinators at BYU. Melanie is not gay and had no real connection to the LGBTQ world until it became part of her work at BYU. She is universally loved by the students she works with. Melanie is also in her forties and has never been married.

For four years, Melanie served as a missionary in a Swahili branch in Utah. She invited me to attend the talk she gave at the end of her mission. I sat next to her mom, who beamed as her daughter spoke. After Melanie's talk, her mom leaned over to me and said, "You know, this wasn't Melanie's plan. She wanted to get married and have ten children. She even chose all their names. We have cried together a lot through the years, and now she has more than ten children. It's amazing how the Lord uses Melanie's pure heart to make the world better." Her mother's words sunk into me. Melanie has experienced tears and pain from unfulfilled dreams, and yet the Lord has taken her on a path that has led her to bless the lives of many—certainly not a path that she would have chosen, but one that blesses her and the world.

As I thought about Melanie's dream to have ten children, I felt sad for those imagined kids because they would have been so lucky to have Melanie as a mom. Then as I was walking across campus one day, I ran into two gay students whom Melanie had taken under her wing. I told them what Melanie's mom had said about her wanting to have ten children. One of the students said, "I don't want to sound selfish, but I'm so glad that didn't happen. If she had gotten married and had that many kids, she wouldn't have time for us." Like her mom said, Melanie has way more children now than just ten. As Elder Maxwell taught, "There is so much to do within what has been allotted to us" ("Content with the Things Allotted unto Us," *Ensign*, May 2000).

On Father's Day I got an unexpected text from Melanie: "I just wanted to thank you for your example of fathering and lifting and mentoring so many. . . . So many younger students look to you for counsel and safety and love and light. You naturally cheer and strengthen wherever you go and radiate Christ in your countenance. Thank you. I am honored to call you one of my dearest friends. You are and will always be a tremendous father, now and in the future . . . in the Church or fostering or adoption . . . whatever ways the Lord has in mind for you. Love and hugs, Melanie." It's funny—until I got this text from Melanie, I hadn't considered that I am a father to many. It was so easy to see how Melanie was a mother, but I didn't see that I was filling this parental role until Melanie pointed it out. My grief over the loss of roles I thought I would have has lessened as I have accepted the roles that God has given me.

While I don't have biological children, I still hope I can be a good dad. I hope that the people in my life feel loved and cared about. Yet even when I'm celebrating the good and feeling so thankful for the life I live, sometimes I still grieve for the life I thought I'd have. And I think that's normal and healthy and okay. These moments happen less and less each year as I focus on what I do have and lean into the roles God has given me. When I was talking to my dad about how he got through his grief, he said, "Being gay has gotten you to where you are." He recognizes that my orientation, this thing that had caused us both to grieve, has been integral in helping me build the beautiful life I have. He told me how proud he was of me, of my life, and of the things I was accomplishing. I asked him how he got to the point of seeing the way my life has unfolded as a blessing. He said, "Lemons turned into lemonade." The lemonade of my life includes the sacred roles I have within my immediate family and the many relationships I treasure with my spiritual siblings, who are part of the family of God.

A BETTER LAND OF PROMISE

How do you plan to move forward with your life?

And finally, in all of living have much of fun and laughter. Life is to be enjoyed, not just endured.
-GORDON B. HINCKLEY, "Stand True and Faithful," *Ensign*, May 1996

September 5, 2017, was the first day of my master's in social work program at BYU. That day I was invited to have lunch with three BYU administrators whom I hadn't previously met. They asked me how it felt being back at BYU. I was honest and told them that I hadn't wanted to come back. I had just finished a PhD in second language acquisition and teaching and had planned on staying in Tucson and working as a Spanish professor. I told them how embarrassing it was to get a PhD in one field and then immediately get a master's in another. I told them that I didn't want to be in school, that I was too old and too tired to do another program. Then I told them that I'd had one of the strongest spiritual promptings I had ever had nudging me to come back to BYU. I said, "I know I need to be a student at BYU right now." One of them looked me in the eye and said that she too believed God had led me there.

I was immediately put to work. While taking a full load of graduate classes and teaching two Spanish classes, my free time was devoted to having discussions and planning events with campus administrators and other LGBTQ students. My first year back at BYU culminated in the campus-wide LGBTQ student forum, which was one of the highlights of my life. I also worked hard to be the kind of teacher I'd want to have. Whenever students came to my office, I'd offer them a snack and a drink and we'd sit and talk about much more than Spanish.

My second year was filled with doing trainings around campus for faculty and staff about how to be inclusive of their LGBTQ students. Those were beautiful and sacred experiences. While doing all this, I was still taking a full load of classes and working as an intern therapist at LDS Family Services in Salt Lake. My supervisor at LDS Family Services took a huge chance on me. He asked me to hold a workshop that local Church leaders could attend on how to minister to their LGBTQ members. He also invited me to train other LDS Family Services therapists in the area. My supervisor was not an overly complimentary person, but he believed in his interns. The day after I gave one of the trainings, he said, "Ben, don't go back to teaching Spanish. Please stay in this field. We need you."

Because of this training, I got to know a number of bishops. They started inviting me to their wards to give lessons on how to minister to our LGBTQ loved ones. I drove up and down I-15 giving lessons and firesides. Each time I spoke, per Church policy, the leader who had invited me needed to get permission from my bishop. He got a lot of calls and emails. One Sunday he asked me if I was getting burned out. I said, "Absolutely not. It's a thrill and an honor every time." I cried tears of gratitude many, many times as I got in my car and drove home alone, thanking Heavenly Father for putting me in a position where I was able to share what

He had taught me. I plan to continue speaking as much as I can in the coming years.

Many of my clients at LDS Family Services self-identified as gay. My office became a sacred space as my clients opened up their hearts and shared their deepest feelings. My clients were different and varied, each in a unique place in life. We talked of moments of spiritual healing. We talked of feelings of anger towards the Church. We talked of deep commitments to the restored gospel. We talked of Church leaders who made mistakes and Church leaders who got things right. We talked of shame and pride and acceptance and self-hatred. We talked of feelings of hopelessness and renewed hope for the future. I always, always, always tried to sit with my clients wherever they were so that they could discover their way forward.

As my social work program came to a close, I remember a distinct moment walking across campus to the Marriott Center for a Tuesday devotional. I realized that BYU had become my home and that I wasn't ready to leave. I felt like I still had more work to do, and more that I could learn at BYU. When an Honor Code administrator position opened up two months after I graduated, I knew I had to apply. Still, I wasn't sure I wanted to stay in Utah. Having spent five years in Arizona, I had developed quite a distaste for winter, and I wasn't sure Utah was where I wanted to put down roots. I drove to the temple the day before my job interview to get some direction and clarity.

I walked up to the Provo City Center Temple praying that I would know if the Honor Code job was the right fit for me. As I entered the building, I was unexpectedly greeted by a friend. She hugged me and asked about my life. I told her about a different job I had just interviewed for, and she was happy for me. Then I said I had an interview the next day to work in the Honor Code

Office at BYU. She nearly lost it—she got so excited. She told me that I had to get the Honor Code job, that it would be perfect for me, and that I would rock at it. I thought, *Wow, I didn't expect that prayer to be answered so quickly and specifically.* As I sat in the temple, I felt that I would be offered the job and that I should accept it.

One of the reasons I applied for the job is because I love LGBTQ BYU students so much. As a student, I worked shoulder-to-shoulder with other LGBTQ students; some of the finest people I've ever met. Over and over again I heard students express fear of the Honor Code Office, almost as if there were Honor Code administrators hiding in the bushes ready to jump out and pounce at the slightest hint of a policy violation. I wanted the Honor Code Office to be more accessible to LGBTQ students instead of the scary, amorphous entity that many perceived it to be. I hoped that my presence in the office could mitigate those fears. So after I got hired, I started taking my LGBTQ friends out to lunch, and I'd have them meet me in my office. This way I could introduce them to my colleagues, and my colleagues would get to meet my gay friends. Some of them became regulars and developed relationships with other members of the staff. Charlie Bird, the famed Cosmo the Cougar mascot who went viral for his incredible dance routines, can't come by without being asked to do some kind of tumbling trick.

Students I didn't know started to set up appointments to talk with me. When they come in, I open up my cupboard and offer them a LaCroix. I tell them it doesn't matter which flavor they choose, because they are all equally tasteless. And then we talk about whatever is on their minds. Students have come in and shared some deeply painful experiences. More than once I've wept with a student in my office. One student came in to tell me that she was going to transfer to a different school because she felt so unwelcome as a gay woman at BYU. I told her, "I want you to be where you will be happy and where you will thrive, wherever that is. And selfishly, I want you here because this university would be poorer without you. I believe LGBTQ students belong at BYU." Other times students come in just asking for life advice. I've talked to students about how to handle having a crush on a roommate or how to come out in a class, and I've talked to many straight students about how they can support their LGBTQ loved ones. I want my office to be a place where any student can come to talk.

The Honor Code Office director, Kevin Utt, often has meetings with LGBTQ students who have questions about BYU policies. He has invited me to participate in almost all of these meetings. I have been impressed with his kindness as I have observed him sincerely trying to understand each student and their unique circumstances. After each meeting (literally every meeting), Kevin and I debrief what was said. He asks for feedback and makes sure that he said the right thing. All of my colleagues in the Honor Code Office have been very supportive of me.

On a Wednesday evening in January 2020, I participated on a campus-wide panel titled "Navigating Faith and Sexuality." Instead of going home after work, almost all of my Honor Code Office colleagues came to hear me speak and sat near the front to cheer me on. The next day some of them had questions about things I had said, and the conversation continued. When I started a podcast with Charlie about LGBTQ topics, they asked for the link so they could listen. When I corrected outdated terminology I overheard, they adjusted and used the terms I recommended. When I was asked to give a talk at a large event, they offered to let me practice on them. I was worried that working in the Honor

Code Office would restrict the ways that I am able to be an advocate, but instead it has opened up more opportunities.

The same week I was hired at BYU, I was also called to be on the high council in my stake. This was not a call I had expected. When he extended the calling, President Bryan Hopkins said, "I want you to know that we're not calling you to be 'the gay high councilor,' but you can talk about being gay as much or as little as you like. We trust you." He also told me that this calling came from the Lord, not from him. Then he said that if any stake members complained that there is an openly gay man on the high council, he would personally talk to them. I love serving in the restored Church, and I cannot envision a future in which I am not fully engaged in building Zion.

Unlike when I accepted a stake calling in Tucson, I didn't cry that night when I wrote in my journal about being called to the high council. Almost five years had passed, and the shame I felt back then was totally gone. This happened as I opened up more, as people began to know all of me, and as I approached God to know how He felt about my orientation. I am no longer ashamed of being gay. There isn't one way to be gay, and there isn't one way to be a Latter-day Saint. I am thrilled to be both gay and a Latter-day Saint because that's who I have felt called to be.

As part of his counsel to his son Helaman, Alma taught how the Liahona had led their fathers to the promised land. He then promised, "For just as surely as this director did bring our fathers, by following its course, to the promised land, shall the words of Christ, if we follow their course, carry us beyond this vale of sorrow into a far better land of promise" (Alma 37:45). I'm grateful that God didn't answer my thousands of prayers to change my orientation. He knew what I needed better than I did. If I had followed the course I had expected, I would have gotten married at twenty-three, had five kids, and been a high school Spanish teacher somewhere in the Seattle area. That would be a beautiful life. But instead, God led me to a better life for me—a better land of promise. A life that I couldn't even have conceived of. And I thank God for the life I have.

If you had told me when I was twenty-six that I'd be where I am, doing what I'm doing at thirty-six, I would've thought you were crazy. The Apostle Paul taught, "Eye hath not seen, nor ear heard, neither have entered into the heart of man, the things which God hath prepared for them that love him" (1 Corinthians 2:9). Joseph Smith wrote, "Ye cannot behold with your natural eyes, for the present time, the design of your God concerning those things which shall come hereafter, and the glory which shall follow after much tribulation" (D&C 58:3). I can't see what the rest of my life will look like. I can't even fully imagine what my life will be like at forty-six, or fifty-six, or beyond, but I have complete confidence that my life will be wonderful.

I sometimes get asked if I'll be gay in the next life. This was once an important question to me and consumed a lot of my mental energy. At times I thought that I would be straight the moment I left mortality, and at other times I thought that being gay was an eternal part of my soul. However, I feel like I was focused on the wrong question. Now I live in the ambiguity and accept that I can't even imagine what the next life will be like. What I do know about my future is summed up by the Apostle John: "Beloved, now are we the sons of God, and it doth not yet appear what we shall be: but we know that, when he shall appear, we shall be like him; for we shall see him as he is" (1 John 3:2). I am a child of God—that I know for sure—but what my sexual orientation (and so many other things) will be like isn't as important as whether or not I'm becoming like the Savior. What I do know is that when Christ appears, I want to be like Him.

President Oaks taught in October 2019, "There is so much we do not know that our only sure reliance is to trust in the Lord and His love for His children." He also quoted an unnamed Church leader who was responding to a family's concerns about what their family would be like in the next life: "You are worried about the wrong things. You should be worried about whether *you* will get to those places. Concentrate on that. If you get there, all of it will be more wonderful than you can imagine" ("Trust in the Lord," *Ensign*, Nov. 2019). The next life is something that I can't even conceive of, but I know that it will be wonderful and glorious. Whether we are gay or straight, our Heavenly Parents have not prepared a sad or disappointing heaven for Their children.

As I look forward to the rest of my life, I am planning on consecrating my time and gifts. I love serving, and I serve others as much as I can. But I don't believe that one type of action or activity can compensate for all of the complex emotional and spiritual needs I have. Running exhaustedly from project to project in order to fill my time is not the answer. After all, the law of consecration isn't only about giving all that we have; it's also about receiving all that others, including God, have to give. Joy in life comes from understanding the balance.

Life is full of ups and downs, highs and lows. I understand that there will be joys even in the times of sorrow. For example, my mom was diagnosed with Alzheimer's in September 2016, and the disease progressed quickly. She no longer knows my name or that I'm her son, but she knows that I'm a person she loves very much. I try to visit my parents in Washington as much as possible so that I can spend time with my mom while also easing my dad's caregiving load. My mom loves to go on walks, so I'll drive us somewhere pretty, put an earbud in each of our ears, and we'll sing songs and dance while we walk down the road. When we get back to the car she often says, "Already? I want to keep going."

When I was visiting home in the summer of 2019, I thought it would be fun to come out to her again. I was a little nervous because I didn't know how she'd react.

"Mom, I'm gay."

"You're . . . gay . . . ," she'd say the words slowly, trying to understand them.

"What do you think about that?" I'd ask.

"Well, as long as you're happy and you get to do the things you like to do."

I've come out to her periodically since then, and that's what she always says: "Do the things you like to do." She just wants me to be happy.

She's not good at answering questions anymore, so now I just tell her things about her life, and she's always delighted.

"Mom, did you know I'm your son?"

"Really?! My son?" she'll say.

"Yep, you actually have four kids. I'm your baby and your favorite." (If there's one thing I'll go to hell for, it'll be constantly messing with my mother and tricking her into saying that I'm her favorite child.)

Once when I told her this, she put her hand on my arm and said, "Thank you for telling me what you told me. I didn't know. I'm just so lucky to have you. You are so nice and so kind to me and just an amazing guy. You are a great son, and there's no one better." Watching my mom deteriorate has been heartbreaking. And yet, in the midst of this terrible disease, we have these beautiful moments. I hope that as I move forward through life I will continue to find peace and joy in the tough moments. Even with a brain that is slowly shutting down, my mom continues to teach me about love and affirmation.

In 2 Peter 1, Peter lists nine Christlike attributes. He then writes: "For if these things be in you, and abound, they make you that ye shall neither be barren nor unfruitful in the knowledge of our Lord Jesus Christ" (2 Peter 1:8). Developing His attributes is one of the ways that we learn about Him. Then Peter says this: "For we have not followed cunningly devised fables, when we made known unto you the power and coming of our Lord Jesus Christ, but were eyewitnesses of his majesty" (v. 16). The stories I have told in this book are not cunningly devised fables, and they are not stories that I have made up. I lived them. Unlike Peter and the ancient Apostles, I have not been an eyewitness of the Resurrection of Jesus Christ. I have not felt the marks of the nails in His hands and His feet or the wound in His side. But I have been an eyewitness of the reality of the Atonement of Jesus Christ and His power to heal and change lives. And I have been an eyewitness that our Heavenly Parents love Their LGBTQ children so very much.

When people ask me what I want my life to look like, I quote for them my favorite scripture. It was penned by Joseph Smith in a letter to the Saints while he was in Liberty Jail: "Therefore, dearly beloved brethren, let us cheerfully do all things that lie in our power; and then may we stand still, with the utmost assurance, to see the salvation of God, and for his arm to be revealed" (D&C 123:17). I used to think that if I did all that I could, God would then reveal His arm. Looking back, He was there all along. In the years to come, I'm going to cheerfully do all that I can in my sphere of influence to build Zion and make the world a better place.

EPILOGUE: RESPONDING TO THE KNOCK AT THE DOOR

What can I do to minister to LGBTQ members of the Church?

If you don't walk as most people do,
Some people walk away from you,
But I won't! I won't!
If you don't talk as most people do,
Some people talk and laugh at you,
But I won't! I won't!
I'll walk with you. I'll talk with you.
That's how I'll show my love for you.
Jesus walked away from none.
He gave his love to ev'ryone.
So I will! I will!
Jesus blessed all he could see,
Then turned and said, "Come, follow me."
And I will! I will!
I will! I will!
I'll walk with you. I'll talk with you.
That's how I'll show my love for you.

–"I'll Walk with You," *Children's Songbook,* 140

I began this book by telling the story of Rhoda and inviting you, the reader, to walk in my shoes. I have purposefully shared stories of how non-LGBTQ people have helped me on my journey to give examples of what others can do. I have been extremely fortunate to have had such loving, wonderful people in my life. I'd like to share one last story that I hope will model the good that an individual can do. This story is about a modern-day Rhoda. It's about a person who answered an unexpected knock at the door, learned something new, and then shared what she learned with people who didn't always believe her. It's about my friend Dianna.

In 2014, I returned to Tucson after spending weeks at my parents' house trying to figure out how to move forward. I had few answers, but one thing I knew was that I needed to stop hiding. I had decided not to force my experiences on anyone, but to be honest with people when my orientation came up organically. Dianna and I had carpooled to a young single adult activity on Mt. Lemmon, just north of Tucson, and as the two of us drove down the mountain I felt a prompting to come out to her. I mentioned our friend Laura whose nickname is Fun Laura. Dianna asked, "Does Fun Laura have a nickname for you?"

I replied, "Yep, she calls me Gay Mormon Ben," to which Dianna responded, "Why does she call you that?" and I said, "Because I am both of those things." Dianna seemed a little stunned by this revelation. I had wanted to tell Dianna I was gay for a long time, and I was glad to finally tell her. She was mostly cool about it, but she lamented that she'd had a crush on me and that she always has crushes on gay guys. I was a little bummed that her initial reaction was to focus on her poor crush choices instead of focusing on me and on our friendship.

Dianna had never had a gay friend before, and she didn't really know what to say at first. I tried to have a conversation about my orientation as we drove, but she didn't seem interested right then. So I just put on some music and we sang songs for the rest of the drive. I brought it up again a few days later, but she really didn't know what to say or how to address the topic. Not long after that, the two of us took the two-hour drive to the Mesa Arizona Temple together. On the drive up, she asked me a question about being gay and that shattered the barrier that had kept us from really talking. We chatted about my experiences the rest of the drive. When we got back in the car, she said she'd been thinking about me the entire time we were in the temple and she had a lot of questions. We talked about faith and sexual orientation for the entire drive home. From that day on, Dianna was committed to being with me on my journey. I had wanted to have this discussion weeks earlier, but Dianna wasn't ready. And that was okay. I have learned that just like it took me years to be ready to explore this reality in my own life, I need to be patient with others and give them time to process their feelings as well.

Six months later, I decided to attend a conference for gay Latter-day Saints in Mesa. I had just barely come out on my blog, and I only had a handful of gay friends. Stepping into the LGBTQ world was terrifying. I wanted to go to the conference, but I didn't want to go alone. I told Dianna I was going, and before I could invite her, she said, "I want to go. Can I go with you?" I wanted to reach out and hug her in that moment for anticipating my need (but I didn't because she's not a huge hugger). Her offer to spend a Saturday with me at a conference was such a gift. While we were at the conference listening to gay Latter-day Saints share their journeys, she would lean over to me and ask, "Did you feel like that?" and I'd say, "Oh, yeah." A few minutes later: "Can you relate to what he's saying?" "For sure." She was walking in my shoes.

When we got in the car, I asked her what she had thought about the conference. She said she needed some time to collect her thoughts. As we sat in the Cafe Rio parking lot a little later, I asked her again. She started to cry. It was one of those rare times when instead of making me feel awkward, the tears felt like a gift. She said that she loves the Church and its doctrines and that she supports our leaders who teach us of the eternal importance of marriage between a man and a woman. She also said that she cares about me and just wishes that I could marry who I want to marry. I wasn't asking Dianna to support same-sex marriage. I wasn't expecting her to change any of her beliefs. I wasn't even asking her to walk in my shoes. All I wanted that day was to not be alone. But she did walk in my shoes, and it expanded her heart.

When I decided to start a support group for LGBTQ Latter-day Saints in Tucson, I didn't even need to ask Dianna if she would be involved. I knew that she would be an ally. She was there at the first meeting when it was just me and two other LGBTQ folks. As the group grew, my house and Dianna's house became LGBTQ Latter-day Saint central in Tucson. People from the group were always hanging out at Dianna's, and she hosted numerous Ally Nights. She was always willing to open her home to the people who needed a place (unless it was late, of course, because Dianna needs her sleep). She often jokingly lamented that her house was always full of boys, but none of them were straight.

Dianna has been an amazing ally as she has supported her LGBTQ friends and helped other people to understand. A month after I moved away from Tucson, Dianna posted the following on the Tucson LGBTQ group Facebook page: "In Relief Society today we had to stand up, say our name, where we're from, and something interesting about us. I took that opportunity to say I'm an ally and anyone can reach out and talk to me. I hope that helps at least one person in the future." I wonder what Dianna from

2014 would think of Dianna now. I bet she never anticipated her life being so full of LGBTQ Latter-day Saints, but that's what happened. Dianna is as committed to The Church of Jesus Christ of Latter-day Saints as anyone I know. I believe that it is because of her commitment to the restored gospel that when she heard the knock at the door, she answered it. And then she helped others see what she had seen. Her faith compelled her to reach out in love and invite others in.

Just like Dianna, many people have answered my knocking and have tried to understand me and my life. Walking in my shoes has led a number of my friends and loved ones to apologize for things they said or did in the past. Usually I don't remember the thing that they're apologizing for, but they remember and feel compelled to tell me they're sorry. Even though the individual apologies have rarely been necessary, the collective amount of them has lifted a weight from me, because I can envision a day when we will no longer say hurtful things to each other. Now when I see someone say or do something that could warrant an "I'm sorry for what I said," I think, *When they know better, they'll do better.* This is not to excuse people who are intentionally hurtful, but to acknowledge that we are all on a journey and I want to offer grace to others who, just like me, are still far from perfection. I'm happy to forgive anyone who wants to be forgiven.

There are people knocking right now, and not just LGBTQ people. People who are married or single. People with children and people without children. People who are overwhelmed with all they have to do and people who are at home alone wishing they had more to do. People who have doubts about their beliefs. People of different ethnic backgrounds and cultures. So many people who just want to be heard and understood. If we are to build Zion, we must create a place where hearts and minds come together and where everyone belongs. This happens as we respond to the knocking we hear, as we throw open the door and welcome people in.

I have one parting request. If you are tempted to give this book to an LGBTQ friend or loved one who has chosen to step away from the Church, I would ask you to resist that temptation and pause for a moment. Instead of giving them my story, can you invite them to tell you theirs?

In Ether 2, the Lord commanded the brother of Jared to build eight barges and then gave very specific instructions on how to accomplish that task. When the brother of Jared was done, he approached the Lord with two remaining problems. The first problem, access to air on their voyage, the Lord solved for him. But the second problem, having light on their journey, He didn't. Instead, He listed some possible solutions that wouldn't work. The Lord then asked him, "What do *you* want me to do?" In chapter 3, the brother of Jared created sixteen transparent stones. He again approached the Lord and asked Him to touch the stones so that they would give light to the Jaredites as they crossed the sea. The Creator of the universe reached out His hand, touched the brother of Jared's creations, and sixteen small stones became sources of light.

Sometimes the Lord has inspired me to do specific things. Other times He has allowed me to come up with a solution. This book is my creation, my sixteen small stones. Sixteen attempts to answer questions about life as a gay Latter-day Saint. I wrote it to address a problem, to help others better understand the LGBTQ Latter-day Saint experience. I have prayed and prayed that this creation of mine would be something that would give more light to the world. And if that is the case, it's not because of me. I know that this book is filled with story after story about me, but it has never been about me. I hope that reading this book has helped you to understand the Atonement of Jesus Christ. I used to think that the Atonement was supposed to make me straight, but instead it healed my broken heart. Writing this book has been a sanctifying process for me, and I hope reading it has brought added light into your life as well. I pray that whatever you are doing with your life, whatever you are creating, the Lord will extend His hand and sanctify your work.

ACKNOWLEDGMENTS

This book would not exist if it weren't for Beth Passey and Tom Christofferson. Two years ago I was talking to Beth on the phone as I swept my kitchen. During the conversation she encouraged me to write a book and promised that she would help me every step of the way. I'd been wanting to write a book for a while, but the project had seemed so huge and so daunting that I hadn't done anything. Yet when Beth made the invitation to help me, I finally felt that I could do it. I didn't write a word for another year, but once I started, she read the first draft of every chapter and gave me valuable feedback. We spent hours together reviewing what I had written and the doctrine I was trying to teach. Beth's influence is all over this book. She made me a promise and she meant it. I can't thank her enough. Tom also encouraged me to write this book and was kind enough to put me in touch with Deseret Book. He believed in this project before it even started.

I want to thank my family and friends for their support. My story is intertwined with the stories of so many others. I'm grateful that my loved ones have allowed me to make public some deeply personal moments that I shared with them. I'm especially grateful to Emma and Jordan for allowing me to write about our romances.

The team at Deseret Book has been immensely helpful. Celia

ACKNOWLEDGMENTS

Barnes took a chance on me and agreed to read my manuscript before we had even met. For months she shared her expertise with me and helped me to write a more concise and compelling narrative. Tracy Keck helped to polish my writing, always insisting that my authentic voice came through. Both women are absolutely delightful to work with and I'm so grateful to them.

So many people assisted me as I wrote. Joey Sheppard regularly reminded me to make writing a priority and to not procrastinate. Stacey Shaw and Eric Hales read the entire first draft and helped me to hone some of my thoughts. Brandie Siegfried read an early draft and reminded me to use my own voice. Charlie Bird provided valuable feedback and advice as we worked on our books at the same time. Heidi Vogeler discussed doctrine with me that I included in the book. My mother, even though she didn't understand what we were doing, sat with me as I read the entire book to her out loud. So did my dad, but he knew what we were doing.

I am deeply grateful for my entire team in the BYU Honor Code Office. I wrote large portions of this book during my downtime at work, and they were always supportive of this project. They celebrated milestones with me and cheered for me when I told them the book had been accepted for publication. They're my colleagues, but more than that, they are my friends.

I'd also like to thank Joleen Rees. In 2008, she encouraged me to start a blog so she could keep up with my life. This gave me seven years of writing experience before I felt a push to start addressing LGBTQ topics in that space. Joleen's invitation helped me become a better writer and storyteller. I still think of her whenever I write a blog post because she was my first audience. Thanks to her, I had already developed a platform for sharing my life when it was time to do so. I didn't realize at the time how important that invitation was, but I'm so glad she extended it.

ABOUT THE AUTHOR

BEN SCHILATY was born and raised in the Seattle area. He currently works as an Honor Code administrator and adjunct professor at Brigham Young University in Provo, Utah. He holds three degrees from BYU: a bachelor's degree in Latin American studies, a master's in Hispanic linguistics, and a master's in social work; he also earned a PhD in second language acquisition and teaching from the University of Arizona. Ben learned Spanish and Portuguese during his mission in Chihuahua, Mexico, and when he lived in Bolivia, Peru, and Portugal. He put his language abilities to good use by teaching Spanish for a decade at middle school, high school, and college levels. Ben's experience as a gay Latter-day Saint prompted him to start a blog and, during his time in Arizona, create a support community for LGBTQ members of The Church of Jesus Christ of Latter-day Saints. He co-hosts the podcast *Questions from the Closet* with his friend Charlie Bird.